New Nations and Peoples

Yugoslavia

Yugoslavia

PHYLLIS AUTY

with 95 illustrations and 2 maps

New York
WALKER AND COMPANY

Contents

1   Cross-roads of East and West

YUGOSLAVIA, founded in 1918 after the First World War, is one of the youngest states in Europe. The seven regions in the Balkan Peninsula which united to form Yugoslavia – Slovenia, Serbia, Croatia, Dalmatia, Montenegro, Bosnia-Hercegovina and Macedonia – had each had very different histories, and all except Montenegro lived for many centuries under foreign rule. They had virtually no historical unity and it may be said that the South Slavs, the Serbs, Croats, Slovenes and Macedonians who inhabited these seven regions, united together not because of, but in spite of their history. Religion has been a dividing not a uniting factor, for amongst the South Slavs there are three major religions – Orthodox, Catholic and Moslem.

Since 1918, the major problem of the state of Yugoslavia has been that of creating a united nation out of people who previously had been separated by geography, divided and sometimes set against each other by historical circumstances and cultural influences. They had never been under one rule. Montenegro, in a limited form but for a long period, and Serbia, in medieval times and in the nineteenth century, had had their own independent states; Croatia too had known a brief period of independence, but that ended in 1102. It is impossible to understand the magnitude of the problems, and difficult to estimate the tremendous achievements that have been made in the short period of less than fifty years since unity, without knowing something about the widely differing historical backgrounds of the regions that today compose the state of Yugoslavia.

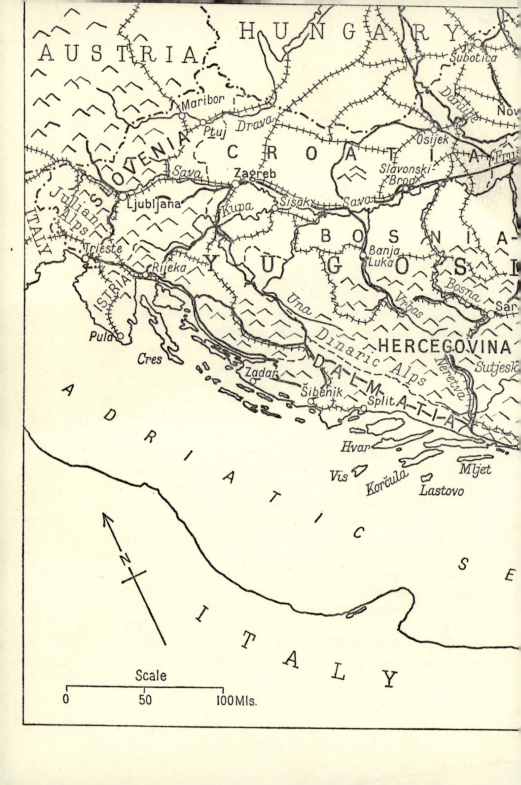

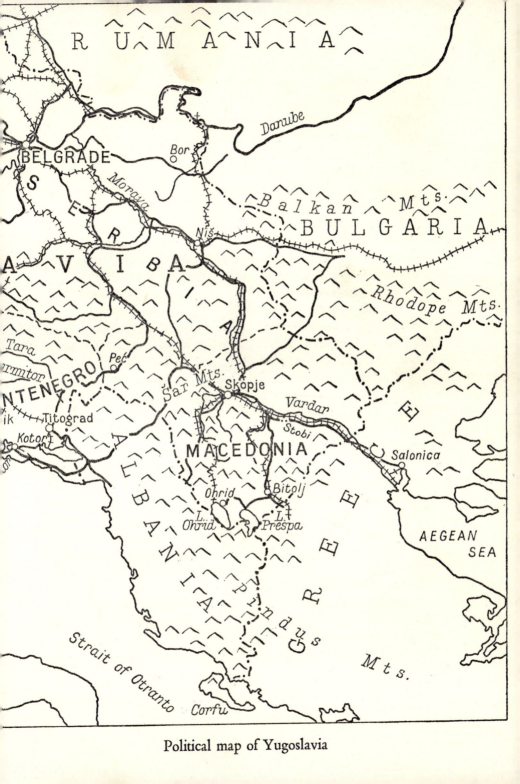

Political map of Yugoslavia

The Balkan Peninsula, of which Yugoslavia occupies the greater part, lies in the borderland between East and West. Throughout history this has been the meeting place for Eastern, Western and Mediterranean cultures, a region which powers from East and West have fought to control. Its inhabitants have experienced the repeated invasion of foreign armies, and the impact of foreign ideas. These lands have been invaded by Greeks, Romans, Barbarians, Byzantines; by armies from Turkey, Austria, France, Russia, Germany. Some parts had close cultural ties with western Europe, other parts were deeply influenced by the Byzantine Empire; later the Turks conquered most of the peninsula and their Moslem rule had a profound effect on the South Slav lands that they occupied. Russia also had an important influence on the southern part of the region through the Orthodox Church, to which both Serbs and Russians belonged, and through help which Russia gave to the Serbs in their struggle to get free from Turkey.

Yugoslavia occupies that part of the Balkans[1] which lies between the Central European Alps and the Pindus mountains of Greece, between the Adriatic Sea on the west, and the foothills of the Balkan and Rhodope mountains on the east. The South Slavs (Jugo= South) who occupy this country today are comparative latecomers to the area; they were not found in great numbers in the Balkans before the fifth and sixth centuries A.D. The original inhabitants of the region were Illyrians and Celts; these were joined by Greeks and Romans who became numerous in the towns during the centuries of Greek and Roman occupation (fifth century B.C. to A.D. 500). In early times the amber trade crossed the Balkans; Phoenicians and Greeks traded along the Dalmatian coast. In the fifth century B.C. Greeks came to settle on the coast and its islands – at Epidauron (Cavtat near Dubrovnik), Iadera (Zadar), Tragurion (Trogir), and other places on the coast, and on islands such as Pharos (Hvar), Corcyra Melaine (Korčula), Issa (Vis).

From Greek remains in museums in Yugoslavia today (in Split, Zagreb, Dubrovnik and other coastal towns) it is clear that Greek trading communities on the Adriatic coastland were prosperous and highly civilized. The fragment of a marble relief of the 'god of the fleeting moment' in Trogir is an exceptionally beautiful example of many such discoveries. We know too that there were extensive Greek settlements in the interior. The museum at Skopje (in spite of the 1963 earthquake) has a rich collection of Greek remains – silver coins, stone capitals and pillars from houses and temples, beautifully decorated vases, jewellery of gold, silver and bronze, statues of Greek gods and a lovely statuette of a dancing Bacchante. These have come from many places – Trebenište, Stobi, Tetovo and Lichnidos (near Ohrid) to mention but a few. Hellenic civilization survived for a long time in this region even after its conquest by Rome.

The Romans had conquered the Balkans by the first century A.D. and created the Roman province of Illyricum. The boundaries of this province were frequently changed, but included Dalmatia which stretched inland as far as Rudnik and had its main city at Salona (present-day Solun near Split), Pannonia which included both banks of the river Sava, with its main town at Petovia (Ptuj in Slovenia), and Moesia which stretched northwards from Macedonia to the Danube and included much of present-day Serbia.

When the Roman Empire was separated into Eastern and Western Empires in 395, the line of division ran through the Balkans separating the Greek-speaking peoples of the south and east, Illyria Graecia, from Illyria Romana in the west and north. This cultural division still existed two hundred years later when the land was settled by the Slavs. It was further emphasized when the Slavs in Illyria Romana were converted to the Christianity of the western Catholic Church, whilst the Slavs of Illyria Graecia, in Serbia, Montenegro, Macedonia and much of Bosnia-Hercegovina, received their Christianity from the Greek Orthodox Church of Constantinople, capital of the Eastern (Byzantine) Empire. Croats and Slovenes became Catholic in religion, Serbs and Macedonians joined the Greek Orthodox Church. The cultural division between these two regions persisted down to our own times.

Roman roads crossed the Balkans from important ports – Aquileia (in Italy today), Split, Durazzo and Salonica. They were paved in stone, had stone bridges and milestones, and were the lines of communication for the Roman legions who manned the many defences.

Amphitheatres for gladiatorial shows for the troops were built in the provinces, as can be seen from the spectacular ruins of the arena at Pula in Istria. There were many towns, busy centres of military and commercial life – Singidunum (Belgrade), Naisus (Niš), Sirmium (Sremska Mitrovica), Aqua Viva (Varaždin) and Siscia (Sisak), to name only a few.

Although few of the present-day towns of Yugoslavia show ruins like those of Pula, yet in the countryside from Ljubljana in the north, to Macedonia in the south, in the Danube and Sava valleys, and on the Dalmatian coast, there are many ruins of Roman occupation. The best known Roman remains in Yugoslavia today are Diocletian's Palace at Split with its vast underground halls, its famous peristyle and temples into whose surrounding walls and area of nine acres a medieval town with houses, shops and Christian churches was crammed in later years.

Diocletian (245–313) was only one of a number of Illyrians who rose through the ranks of the Roman army to become Emperors – there were also Decius and Probus from Pannonia, Claudius from Dardania, Aurelian from Sirmium, Galerius from Serdica, Constantine the Great from Naissius and Jovianus from Singidunum.

From the second century A.D. the Roman Empire was on the defensive against the Barbarians. By the fourth century barbarians had penetrated the Balkans. Goths (under Alaric), Huns (under Attila), plundered and destroyed many Roman towns. Later came other tribes – Ostrogoths, Gepids, Sarmatians, Bulgars and Avars. The Slavs, who are frequently mentioned by the famous Greek writer the Emperor Constantine Porphyrogenitus, first came into the Balkans as foot-soldiers in the armies of the Bulgars and Avars. The Slavs were described as skilled in making and manning special boats made from a hollowed tree-trunk and called monoxyla. These they used to help the Barbarians to cross the Danube river and in the Avar attack on Constantinople in 626. The attack failed and shortly after the Avars themselves disappeared from history. In the sixth century the Slavs entered the Balkans in great numbers bringing their families and possessions. The Byzantine Emperor at Constantinople claimed suzerainty over the Balkan lands and encouraged the Slavs to settle and defend this territory. Soon they ceased to be nomads, built themselves wooden houses and began animal and crop farming.

It is not certain why the Slavs left their original homeland beyond the Carpathians (in the southern part of what is now Poland and the Ukraine) but they were probably forced to move by population explosion and the increased pressure of other nomadic tribes in the area. By the seventh and eighth centuries Slavonic tribes (mentioned by different chroniclers under different names – Venedi, Sclavi, Schiavoni) had settled roughly in the same Balkan regions they now occupy, that is Slovenes and Croats in the northern part, Croats in Dalmatia, and Serbs in the central and southern part of the peninsula.

The Illyrians and Celts were absorbed by the Slavs or fled to the mountains and coastlands. Descendants of the Illyrians who were not absorbed are the present-day inhabitants of Albania. There were also Romanized Illyrians who never adopted the Slavonic language; these were the Vlachs whose descendants, in diminishing numbers, still remain as nomadic herdsmen in the mountains of Macedonia. Roman civilization continued in existence longest in the coastal towns; many of its attributes were inherited and continued by the newcomers who came to live there.

Our knowledge about the early Slavs at the time of their settlement in the Balkans is very scanty.[2] We know that the Slavs settled in the Balkans in more or less tribal groups, that districts occupied by such groups were from early times called *županije* and were often named after rivers or mountains. The head of the group was the *Župan* (duke). At first there were no kings. By the eleventh century class distinctions based on landholding and relationship to the leading families had begun to appear – *Voivoda* was the title of a military leader, *Knez* of a noble.

The basic family unit, typical of the South Slavs had already appeared by this time. This was the *zadruga*, a family group of father, brothers, sons (all with wives and children), living together in one large house or group of buildings. They held land and accepted social responsibilities (taxes for example) in common, and lived and worked communally under the authority of the oldest male – sometimes the oldest female – of the group. Zadrugas, which were found in Serbia and Croatia varied greatly in numbers, often from fifteen to twenty-five persons, but in some recorded cases numbering one hundred people. The zadruga was popular for the protection it gave during times of trouble and for the economic benefits of communal ownership, working arrangements and eating. They were recognized by law and continued to exist throughout the Middle Ages and the period of Turkish occupation, being dissolved as a legal entity finally in 1868. In remote parts of Yugoslavia until 1945 it was still possible to come across zadrugas, despite dissolution.

Christianity had been fairly widespread in the Balkans in Roman times before the coming of the Slavs. St Paul preached in Macedonia, his pupil Titus in Dalmatia. Many of these early Christians were martyrs during the reign of the Emperor Diocletian. The persecution of Christians ended in the fourth century A.D. Disputes followed between the Christians of the eastern Church (of Constantinople) and the western Church (of Rome) and when the Slavs came to the Balkans they settled in the borderland between the two Churches' spheres of influence and were converted by both.

For a long time the religious situation amongst the South Slavs was confused; eastern and western Churches continued to exist side by side although the Greek Orthodox Church was predominant amongst Serbs, the Catholic Church strongest amongst Croats and Slovenes. In Bosnia, inland from the coast, it is possible that in the heretical Christian sect of Bogomils (or Patarines) the influence of early Christianity survived.

Unique amongst ancient remains to be seen in present-day Yugoslavia are the Stečaci (Stečak in the singular), the huge marble gravestones to be found in lonely burial grounds on the plateaux and mountain sides in Bosnia and Hercegovina. They are generally thought to be Bogomil tombstones, but some historians question this, believing that they are more probably an art-form peculiar to the region, not to a particular sect. The tombstones vary greatly in shape and size but are usually in the form of a small stone house, a mausoleum with flat or pointed roof, decorated with striking pictures or patterns in relief.

Mention must be made of the work of the two famous Christian missionaries, Saints Cyril and Methodius. These brothers were sons of a Greek officer in the Byzantine Empire. The younger, Constantine, later to be known as St Cyril, was a librarian and teacher of philo/sophy in the school at the Byzantine Emperor's palace in Constan/tinople, the elder known under his monk's name of Methodius was mayor of a town in Macedonia before he joined an Orthodox monastic order. In 862 some North Slav leaders asked for Christian missionaries to be sent to convert their people and organize a Church. The two brothers were chosen for this task. They worked out a written form of the Slavonic language into which the church books were translated for their missionary work. This written language is known today as Glagolitic and remained the written form of the Serbo/Croat language until a more modern form of written language was worked out by Vuk Karadjić at the beginning of the nineteenth century. The written form of the Slavonic language of Cyril and Methodius used Greek lettering which is now called Cyrillic. In those parts of Yugoslavia today where inhabitants have belonged to the Orthodox Church (Serbia, Montenegro and Macedonia), Cyrillic lettering is still used; in the parts that adhered to the Catholic Church the Latin alphabet is used. The same language – Serbo/Croat – is thus written in two different alphabets; most important books, magazines and newspapers, are printed today in separate editions in both scripts.

Economic map of Yugoslavia

1a By the fifth century B.C. the Greeks had established themselves in the Balkan Peninsula formerly inhabited by Celts and Illyrians. This is a fragment of a Greek marble relief representing the 'god of the fleeting moment' found in Trogir.

1b Also dating from this period is a statuette in bronze of a dancing Bacchante.

2 The Romans occupied and conquered the Balkans in the first century A.D. Their main lines of communication were the many stone roads and bridges which they built. This bridge is at Mostar in Bosnia-Hercegovina.

3 Gladiatorial shows were provided for the troops in amphitheatres. The arena at Pula is one of the finest surviving examples.

4 The Temple of Augustus at Pula.

5 A mosaic floor of an ancient house at Pula also dating from the Roman period.

6 Diocletian was one of the many Illyrians who rose through the ranks of the Roman army to become Emperor. This is part of a marble statue found at Nicomedia.

7 His palace at Split reflects much of the grandeur of the Roman Empire and dates from the third century A.D.

8, 9 The grounds covered an area of nine acres, and in later years a medieval town with houses, shops and Christian churches was crammed within its walls.

ОНѢЖЕКЬ ТРОИЦИ ПОКЛАННѢМЇН
БГЬ БЛГОИЗВОЛИ ИСПЛЬНИТИСЕВО
ЮЦРКВЕ, РАЗЛИЧНЫМИКНИГАМИ
ВИДѢВЬ АЗЬВЬ Х̃А БГА БЛГОВѢРН
ЫИ НѢМЬХРАНИМИ ГИЬ ГЮРГЬЦЕ
РНОЕВЫКЬ· ЦРКВЫ ПРАЗДНЫСТЫХ
КНИГЬ, ГРѢХЬ РА̃ДИ НАШИХ РАЗХЇ
ЩЕНИЕМЬ ИРАЗДРАНИЕМЬ АГАРАНСКЫХЬ ЧЕДЬ · СЬЗРѢ
ВНОВАХЬ ПОСПѢШЕНИЕМЬ СТ̃ГО Д̃ХА, ИЛЮБОВИЮКЬ БЖ
ТВНЫМ ЦРКВАМ · ИНАПИСАХ СИЮ Д̃ШЕСП̃СНУЮКНИГУ Ѽ
МО̃ГЛАСНЫКЬ· ВЬ ИСПЛЬ НЫНИЕСЛАВОСЛОВИЮ Т̃РИСЛИЧНУ Н А̃
ОВЬ Е̃ ДИНСТВѢ ПОКЛАННѢМАГО БЖ̃СТВА · МЛ̃ЮЖЕ ЮНИЕ
ИСЬВЬЗРАСТНЫЕ ИСТАРИЕ, УБѢ ТОЩЕИ ИЛИВЬСПѢВАЮЩЕИ
ИЛИПИШУЩЕЛЮБВЕХ Х̃ВѢ РА̃ДИ НИСПРАВЛАТИ · НАСЖЕ О̃У̃СЬ
РДНЕПО ТЬЩАВШИХСЕ НАСИ Е̃ Ч̃ ЛОБ̃ЛСВЛАТИ · ДА̃ЦБОИ
СЛАВѢЩЕ Ѽ Ц̃А ЗН̃ ЕГОЖЕ ВЬ СА̃ СН̃ АИМЖЕ ВЬ СА̃ · СТ̃ГО Д̃ХА
Ѿ НИ̃ЕМЖЕ ВЬ СА̃ · ЗДѢ О̃У ЛУЧИММ МЛ̃СТЬ ТАМОЖЕ СѢНСВѢ
ТОМ Ѽ ЗАРЫМСЕ, А̃МИН · ПОВЕЛѢНИЕМ ГИ̃А МИ̃ГЮРГИ
ЦЕ РНОЕВИКИ АЗЬ Х̃УРАБЬ СЩ̃ЕНОИНОКЬ МАКА̃ ÏЕ, РОУКО
ДЕ ЛИСАХ СÏЕ· ПРИ ВСЕ Ѽ СЩ̃ЕННОМ МИ̃Т̃РОПОЛИТЕ ЗѢТС
КОМКУ̃Р ВАВУЛЕ· ВЬЛѢТО · З̃А КР̃Г СЛ̃НЦ, А̃ · ЛУНЕ, Ѿ

10 This page from an early Christian hymnbook is written in a Slavonic language
known today as Cyrillic and was invented by Saints Cyril and Methodius, two
ninth-century missionaries.

11 The Slavs were influenced either by the Orthodox or by the Catholic Church. A thirteenth-century wall painting representing the Nativity at the Serbian Orthodox Monastery at Sopočani.

12 These marble gravestones known as the Stečaci are generally thought to belong to the early heretical Christian sect of Bogomils (or Patarines).

13 A family community or *zadruga* consisted of between fifteen and twenty-five people living under the same roof, and this form of communal ownership lasted for centuries. A drawing of a homestead in Slavonia dates from the beginning of the nineteenth century.

2   The Republics and their Past

THE SOUTH SLAVS had no unified history before the unification of 1918. Each region had its own unique history. Thus it is necessary to give a separate account of the regions that today form the six auto' nomous republics of the federal state of Yugoslavia; these are Serbia (including Vojvodina and Kosovo Metohija), Croatia (including the ancient province of Dalmatia), Slovenia, Bosnia'Hercegovina, Montenegro and Macedonia.

SERBIA

Serbia, the largest (34,107 square miles) of the Yugoslav federated republics, was the only region to achieve in medieval times a lasting independent state; it was also the only region to become a fully fledged independent kingdom in the nineteenth century. This past independence has always been a proud memory for Serbs; it has had an important influence on their history.

In the centuries following the Serbian settlement of the central Balkans, two rudimentary states emerged – Duklja (or Dioclea) in the area of present'day Montenegro, and Raška (or Rascia) in today's south'west Serbia. The Byzantine Empire had suzerainty over both provinces. This was less effective in the inland mountain region of Raška which could not be reached from the Adriatic coast. Byzantium, and the powerful medieval state of Bulgaria fought many wars to try to subdue and control the two provinces.

By the middle of the twelfth century Byzantium was weak, Bulgaria in decline had ceased to be a danger, and a powerful

Serbian family called Nemanja had emerged in Raška. In 1168 the Byzantine emperor gave large tracts of land to several Nemanja brothers to hold as vassals of Byzantium. Gradually the two provinces and scattered estates developed into a Serbian state ruled by the foremost member of the Nemanjić family which ruled Serbia until the middle of the fourteenth century.

Serbia became a prosperous and highly developed feudal state. Its frontiers were extended, though incessant fighting was necessary to maintain authority over its widespread territories, stretching northwards to the rivers Sava and Danube, west to the Adriatic coast, east to the river Morava, and, in the fourteenth century, south down the Vardar valley towards the Aegean Sea. The last great Nemanjić king, Stephen Dušan (1331-55) made his capital at Skopje in present-day Macedonia, and aimed to conquer the Byzantine Empire. He died in 1355 whilst assembling an army to attack Constantinople.

Serbian institutions and cultural development owed much to Byzantine influence. The most enduring result seen in our own time is the continued use in Serbia of the Cyrillic (Greek characters) alphabet. The Orthodox religion of the great majority of Serbian people today is also part of the Byzantine legacy. In early years the Catholic religion, spreading from Italy and Hungary, had some influence in Serbia, but this gradually declined. The Orthodox faith became the official religion and bishops and priests were closely associated with the monarchy in establishing a state based on the rule of law and Christian ethics.

At first the Serbian church came under the Bishop of Ohrid (today in Yugoslavia, at that time in Byzantium), but as Serbian rulers became more powerful they wished to have their own independent church. An independent Serbian archbishopric was established in 1219 with its centre at the monastery of Žiča whose ruins can still be seen near the present-day town of Rankovičevo (between Belgrade and Skopje). The first archbishop was St Sava, brother of Stephen the first crowned king of Serbia. For reasons of piety and in order to establish royal authority the Nemanjić kings gave extensive lands to the Orthodox Church. Through its many churches and monasteries, their patronage allowed the church to become wealthy and powerful, a cultural and civilizing influence throughout Serbia. Some idea of the magnificence of this culture can still be seen even today in the beautiful frescoed churches and monasteries (Studenica, Sopočani, Peć and many others) that have survived Serbia's subsequent turbulent history.[3]

Before the sea-routes round Africa were discovered at the end of the fourteenth century, trade with the Far East followed land routes to the great entrepôt of Constantinople; from there caravan routes crossed the Balkans through Serbia, north to central Europe and Venice, and west to Dubrovnik. A map of the medieval trade routes shows a communications system through Serbia more dense than the road system of the early twentieth century.

Serbia grew rich on transit trade (as is evident from the opulence of the churches noted above) and found ready markets for its own exportable goods – wax, honey, skins, sheep and cattle, as well as gold, silver and iron ore. Monastic chronicles as well as trade and diplomatic agreements with neighbouring states and the accounts of Byzantine, Venetian and Dubrovnik writers have left plenty of records of medieval Serbia. The most interesting document illustrating life in Serbia at that time is the Code of King Stephen Dušan which was issued in 1349 and re-issued with additions and emendations in 1354.[4] It gives a vivid impression of feudal society in medieval Serbia at its highest point.

Three years after emending his code, Stephen Dušan died without leaving an able successor, and medieval Serbia rapidly disintegrated. It is idle to speculate what might have happened had Serbia produced another great king, but it is doubtful if it could have survived. The downfall of medieval Serbia was caused by the Turkish invasion of the Balkans. This had begun before the end of Dušan's reign. It was helped because the Balkan states and their neighbours were not prepared to sink their rivalries and make common cause to keep the Turks out of Europe. Hatred between Catholic states (Hungary, Austria and Venice) and Orthodox states (Byzantium, Serbia and Bulgaria) was as great as that between Christian and Turk.

Year after year in the fourteenth and fifteenth centuries the Turks invaded the Balkans. Serbia was defeated at the Battle of Maritsa in

1371 and destroyed in the famous Battle of Kosovo in 1389. In this battle both the Turkish Sultan Murad and the Serbian leader, Prince Lazar, were killed. The tomb of the Sultan can still be seen in Kosovopolje. The Serbian nobility was virtually eliminated as a result of this battle. Those who were left either fled abroad or lost their estates and noble status in the ensuing Turkish occupation.

For hundreds of years the battle of Kosovo remained a memory of almost mystical importance for Serbian people; its traumatic significance is only beginning to wane in our own times. Kosovo was the subject of heroic ballads sung by a minstrel, or *guslar*, who played a mournful accompaniment on a single-stringed instrument the *gusle*. Vidovdan, or St Vitus day, on which the battle was fought was until recently preserved as a national holiday.

The last remnant of Serbia, the Despotate of Smederevo on the Danube was captured in 1459. The surrounding provinces fell to the Turks one by one – Bosnia in 1463, Hercegovina in 1482, Montenegro in 1499. The Turks also captured much of the mainland of Dalmatia (but in spite of repeated attempts, not the free city of Dubrovnik); Belgrade fell in 1521. Croatia and Hungary were then at the mercy of the Turks. Hungary was captured after the débâcle of the Battle of Mohacs in 1526, and with Croatia, remained under Turkish rule until the end of the seventeenth century. Serbia did not regain its freedom until a hundred years later.

When the Turks first occupied Serbia their rule was not so harsh, nor were they so hated as in later years. In all major conquering battles they were helped by some Serbs, amongst them notable figures such as Marko Kraljević whose legendary exploits, both with and against the Turks, are another popular subject in the heroic ballads. Turkish government was at first more efficient, stable and less oppressive than rule in Serbia had been under the successors of Stephen Dušan. The misrule and tyranny, however, which characterized the latter period of Turkish rule were long remembered whilst the better side of their rule was often unrecorded.

For administrative purposes the Turkish empire was divided into *sanjaks* (a name preserved in modern times in the Sanjak of Novi Pazar); in later years these were grouped into *beglerbegs* or *pashaliks*

28

under the rule of a *beg* or *pasha*. The pasha had his own advisory council, the *divan*, and his own chief justice, the *kadi*. The basis of Turkish rule was the Koran, and Moslem law and practice deriving from it. Christians and other non-Moslems could not have any of the privileges of citizenship. Slavs who refused to become Moslems – and in Serbia this meant the majority of the people – thus became the serfs (or *rayah*) of the Turkish empire. This abolished the class system of medieval Serbia and is the reason why (in spite of inevitable inequalities that developed over the years) there were no large landowners or significant class distinctions amongst the Serbs when they finally regained their freedom in the nineteenth century.

According to Turkish belief all conquered land belonged to God which in earthly terms meant the Sultan. Land in the Balkans was assigned in fiefs (*timars*) of varying sizes to Moslem – and very occasionally Christian – knights on condition of military service. Tenancies were not hereditary in theory but were usually so in practice. The knights, called *spahis*, had to give personal service and provide an agreed number of *kilics* (sabres) for the Sultan's army. They received a tenth (sometimes more) of the produce of the land farmed by the rayah, the Serbian peasants. Spahis also had to see that part of the income from the land was collected in the form of taxes for the Sultan.

The spahis lived in towns, where they could readily be called up, and where Turkish life and comforts could be most easily protected. A house was kept on the spahi's lands where he or his representative received the peasants' tenths which included tenths of grain, orchards, beehives, pigs, water, as well as an assessed tax at marriage and death. In addition the rayah did a number of days forced labour both for the Sultan and for the spahi and paid a tax in money to the Sultan which in Serbia was levied as a poll-tax called *harač*.

In early days of Turkish rule the amount of produce, taxation and forced labour for Serbian peasants was less than the feudal exactions from peasants in many other parts of Europe. But the Turks imposed also a unique and much hated levy of male children for the Turkish army. Each year from one district or another, a number of the healthiest boys between ten and twenty years old were seized and taken to Turkey to be converted to Islam, educated and trained for the *élite* corps of 'new' soldiers, the *janissaries*. The last levy in Serbia was in 1638, but the memory of the horrible custom (preserved in epic ballads) remained bitterly present for many years after it had been abandoned.

At first the Turks had little direct contact with the Serbs, who were allowed to live in their own communities, running their own patriarchal local government. The zadruga, or large family group living in one homestead, became an entrenched institution for it facilitated both tax collection and local government. All official business with the Turks was transacted through village headmen, and no attempt was made to assimilate or proselytize. The few who converted to Islam were given immediate privileges, but most Serbs resisted this temptation. For the rest, the humiliations of being a conquered people were ever present though there is plenty of evidence that many Serbs managed both to remain Christian and become prosperous under Turkish rule.

One of the most deeply resented aspects of Turkish rule – especially to those Serbs who prospered through trades which Moslems were too idle or inhibited by their religion to practise – were the regulations designed to enhance the prestige of the ruling class. Serbs were forbidden to possess arms, to ride on horseback in the presence of Turks, to wear fine clothes; any Turk could force a rayah to do degrading services for him. Punishment for those who transgressed was savage. Serbs who fell foul of Turkish law often became bandits operating in the mountains aided by the local population. This was the origin of the *hajduk*, the hero whose exploits became the subject of many popular epic ballads.

Perhaps the worst result of Turkish rule in Serbia was the lack of political or economic development. Serbs were cut off from contact with the main developments of the rest of Europe. Their customs became embalmed in a deep inward-turning, excessively proud nationalism. Trade routes no longer passed through Serbia, economic improvement was discouraged through lack of incentives and crippling taxation.

The Orthodox Church played an important part in preserving the spirit of Serbian nationalism. Though the Church lost its independence in 1459 when it was incorporated into the Patriarchate of Constantinople, it was still allowed to function on a village level. Priests lived like peasants, largely uneducated except for basic ritual training and tilling the soil themselves; only a few managed to be educated abroad. Although the Serbian Church was allowed to have its own Patriarchate again in 1557 its power was very limited and it declined as a cultural centre until it was abolished in 1766.

The Orthodox Church came to be synonymous with Serb nationalism.[5] Orthodox priests were leaders (often fighting) of revolts against Turkish rule. These were many, but they were usually local and easily suppressed. Some Serbs sought to escape by migrating from the Turkish lands across the Danube and Sava rivers into Austria. This was an almost continuous economic and political movement throughout the Turkish period. The biggest migration was in 1691 when the Serbian Patriarch Arsen III led about 30,000 Serbs (estimates of the numbers vary) into Austria. The Catholic Habsburg emperors welcomed these Orthodox refugees, allowing them freedom to practise their religion. They were settled in the depopulated areas of the Austro-Hungarian Empire (especially in regions that the Turks were forced to surrender at the end of the seventeenth century) and became the soldier peasants of an Austrian Military Frontier District organized along the border with the Ottoman Empire. These were the ancestors of the *prečani* ('across the river') Serbs who today inhabit parts of Croatia and the Vojvodina north of Belgrade. There were other migrations during the Turkish period which had important results for Serbia. People tended to leave the river valleys where armies operated and go to live in the inaccessible mountain lands which became over-populated and have remained so down to our own times.

A great change came over Turkish government in Serbia in the late seventeenth and eighteenth centuries. This was due to many complicated causes – decline in the authority of Turkish central government over outlying provinces, decline due to economic weakness when Turkey was no longer expanding and had to bear the expense of fighting repeated wars against the growing power of

Austria. By the treaty of Passarowitz (Požarevac) 1718, Austria regained most of Hungary and Croatia.

By the middle of the eighteenth century Russia had also begun to take an active interest in the fate of the Slav peoples of the Balkans. Russian people were Slav by race, and Orthodox in religion. South Slavs and Russians could understand each other's language and with these bonds of affinity were ready to use each other for political ends. During this century Russia evolved a policy which she was to follow throughout the nineteenth century. It was a policy in Asia of wresting from Turkey lands conquered in early centuries, and in Europe to push Turkey out of the Balkan provinces.

A first step was taken during the wars between Russia and Turkey in the reign of Catherine the Great (who had ambitious but un-realized plans for the liquidation of Turkey by division between Russia and Austria). By the Treaty of Kutchuck Kainardji (1774), Turkey gave Russia the right to 'protect' Orthodox subjects of the Sultan. After this it was only a matter of time before Russia was in a position to help the Serbs to revolt against Turkey.

Changes brought by the French revolution and Napoleonic wars provided a local and international situation favourable to revolt. Napoleon had invaded the Turkish provinces of Egypt and Syria, and Turkey was fearful of his further intentions. Russia, taking advantage of Turkey's weak position had occupied Moldavia and Wallachia, Turkish provinces adjacent to Serbia. Unrestrained by the Sultan, local Turkish officials and mutinous Turkish soldiers had for some years been committing outrages of tyranny against Serbian peasants. The time was ripe for revolt. The Serbian uprising began in 1804 in the district of Šumadija, south of Belgrade. Its leaders were local heads of families (now called *kneževi* or princes) who appointed their own military leaders (*vojvoda*) and were soon sup-ported by the entire Serbian peasant population of the Pashalik of Belgrade. The elected leader was Djordje Petrović, known as Karadjordje (black George); he was a fairly prosperous pig-trader (proving that not all Serbian rayah were tied to the soil in grinding poverty at this time), who had at one time migrated across the river and served in the Austrian army.

The rebels appealed for help to both Austria and Russia. Though they received financial aid from the latter, and considerable support in money and arms from Serbs living in Austria, the success of the first revolt was due to the courage and vigour with which the Serbs attacked a weakened Turkey. By 1808 the Pashalik of Belgrade had been conquered, and Serbian independence won.

Success was short-lived, for when Napoleon invaded Russia in 1812, all Russian troops were withdrawn from eastern Europe. Other powers were preoccupied with plans for Napoleon's overthrow, and Turkey was free to deal with her rebellious subjects. In 1813 the Serbs were defeated. Their leaders were killed, or, like Karadjordje, forced to flee to safety in Austria. Turkish rule was reimposed with savage ferocity.

A minor leader who stayed behind, a village headman adept at negotiating with the Turks, was Miloš Obrenović. When Turkish reprisals became too ferocious, he led a second revolt in 1815. The French danger in Europe was over; Russia, though weakened by military losses, was at last free to aid the Serbs by diplomatic pressure on Turkey. After 1816, Serbia, though still a province of Turkey, became virtually independent.

By the Treaty of Adrianople (1829) Turkey granted Serbia autonomy, and Russia received the right to protect Orthodox Christians in Serbia. Turkish *hatti sharifs* of 1830 and 1833 regulated other matters, most important of which were that Miloš Obrenović was recognized as Prince of Serbia (Karadjordje had been murdered with Miloš' connivance when he returned to Serbia in 1818): Turkish military fiefs and landholdings (other than fortresses and town property in Serbia) were abolished.

Miloš Obrenović had many important decisions to make when Serbia became free. One of these was the question of whether to create a class of large landholders amongst his own people or to give the Serbian peasants the land which Turks had surrendered. Needing popular support he chose the latter course so that no upper landowning class was re-created in Serbia. It remained a country of small landholders with a fairly egalitarian class structure. Exceptions there were, for Miloš, following the Turkish customs, used his position to enrich himself and his family both as a landowner and by trade monopolies and bribes for government contracts. His example was followed by politicians and public servants throughout the history of Serbia, establishing an unfortunate tradition of government corruption which persisted until the Second World War. Serbia did not obtain complete freedom from Turkey until 1878 (Treaty of Berlin); its prince took the title of king in 1881.

There were many problems to be solved in Serbia in the nineteenth century. The country was small and did not include all areas occupied by Serbs, many of whom lived in Montenegro, south Serbia, Bosnia-Hercegovina and Macedonia. Almost all Serbs, including the prince, were illiterate. In such conditions the organization of a new state was extremely difficult and was only achieved with considerable aid from the educated and more experienced Serbs of Austria-Hungary, the most famous of whom was Vuk Karadjić. He worked out a system of orthography and made a written collection of the epic ballads which up to that time were only an oral tradition.

A further difficulty which weakened public life in Serbia was the bitter rivalry between the descendants of Karadjordje and those of Miloš Obrenović. Both families claimed the hereditary right to rule Serbia, and both provided Serbian rulers during the nineteenth century. Neither family produced an outstanding political personality and the threat of murder was ever present. Michael Obrenović was murdered in 1867 and the Obrenović family was finally liquidated by the murder of Alexander Obrenović who died without heirs in 1903. He was succeeded by Peter I, a Karadjordjević who ruled Serbia till the outbreak of the First World War. His descendants were accepted as rulers of Yugoslavia up to the Second World War.

During the last quarter of the nineteenth century Serbia developed rapidly. But its constitutional government, based on western models, with political parties and an elected parliament, disguised the fact that government was not really democratic. Though the majority of people, and some of the deputies, were peasants, executive power was in the hands of a very small group of townspeople, politicians who largely served their own interests or those of a small minority. The king's powers, though limited, were still large and were exercised by a dangerously chauvinistic military clique. Most of these conditions, the source of much general dissatisfaction, persisted after Serbia had been incorporated into the Kingdom of Yugoslavia.

Foreign relations, especially with the Great Powers Austria and Russia were of crucial importance throughout Serbia's history as an independent state. Although small and weak, Serbia (that is her rulers and politicians) had ambitious aims. From the time of Prince Miloš until 1914 foreign policy was for national expansion – to extend Serbia's frontiers to include all Serbs and kindred people, but not at this stage Croats and Slovenes. This meant that she aimed to take over Bosnia-Hercegovina and large tracts of Macedonia from Turkey as soon as opportunity presented itself. This ambition clashed with Austrian and Russian wishes to control these same areas.

In 1866 Austria was defeated by Prussia and thereafter lost all power and influence in Germany. As a result Austrian ambitions in the Balkans were strengthened, for some politicians and soldiers believed that control of Bosnia-Hercegovina and of Macedonia with the port of Salonica would restore the diminished power of the Habsburg empire. Russia was strongly opposed to this; she considered the Balkans with its Slav and Orthodox population as her sphere of influence. If Turkey was disintegrating into its component parts Russia was determined that she and not Austria should control any new Balkan states.

At first Serbia thought that Russia would help her to realize her ambitions in order to keep Austria out of the Balkans. But Serbia's rulers proved too independent and nationalistic for the Russians. After defeat in the Crimea, Russia realized that she could not force solution of the Balkan problems without making some concession to Austria, and ultimately agreed that Bosnia-Hercegovina should be an Austrian sphere of influence. Serbia was bitterly disappointed by this decision for without Russian support she could not oppose Austria. Matters reached a crisis when during the Russio-Turkish war (1877–8) a revolt of Christian peasants flared up against Turkish rule in Bosnia-Hercegovina. Prolonged negotiations between Austria, Russia and Turkey failed to produce agreement about a peaceful solution. Other European powers became involved.

35

Britain, and especially her Premier Disraeli, was anxious to keep Turkey intact as a check on expanding Russian power.

In 1877 Russian troops invaded Turkey and advanced to within sight of Constantinople, but fighting was stopped by the threat that Britain would enter the war on Turkey's side. Victorious Russia pro-posed a peace treaty (at San Stefano, 1878) setting out a settlement. Bosnia and Hercegovina were to be occupied by Austria, the Bulgarian people (hitherto under Turkey) were to be freed and given a large state which would have stretched across Macedonia as far as Albania, including in the south part of the Aegean coast and reaching the outskirts of the port of Salonica. Russia intended that the new Bulgaria should be a puppet state under her control. These proposals enraged Serbia and were equally displeasing to Austria, who saw her ambitions in the southern Balkans thwarted.

The treaty never took effect. It was replaced by the Treaty of Berlin (1878) which created a small independent Bulgaria, gave a great part of Macedonia back to Turkey and allowed Austria to occupy Bosnia-Hercegovina. Although Serbia became an independent kingdom and gained from Turkey a small extension of her southern frontier, the treaty was a bitter disappointment for her. It brought Austria into the Balkans and the whole affair had shown that Russia preferred to give support to Bulgaria.

The Treaty of Berlin did not bring peace to the Balkans. It set Bulgaria and Serbia against each other – and Bulgarians did not forget that San Stefano had virtually established for them a claim to rule all Macedonia. It satisfied Austria but did not satisfy Russia, and it left the Slav inhabitants of Bosnia-Hercegovina under foreign rule. Abandoned by Russia, Serbia turned to Austria to see what she could get by working with, rather than against her great neighbour. This policy lasted until 1891, but Serbia's rulers and people found that being a puppet state under Austrian dominion restricted their freedom, especially in matters of commerce.

Serbian ambitions had been frustrated but not extinguished. King Milan abdicated in 1889 and was succeeded by his son Alexander who was even less popular than his father. King Alexander, a despotic psychopath, was murdered by a group of Serbian military officers in 1903 and succeeded by Peter Karadjodjević I who ruled until the outbreak of war in 1914. He restored good relations with Russia. Hostility against Austria (who had demonstrated that she was determined to dominate Serbia) and the aim to gain the other Slavonic provinces were of overriding importance in these years. This was the policy of the army officers who had murdered Alexander and who controlled his successor.

After 1903 military preparations became paramount. The annexation of Bosnia-Hercegovina by Austria-Hungary in 1908 did little more than give legal sanction to a situation that already existed, but it enraged Serbian politicians. By 1912 they had built up alliances with Greece and Bulgaria (patching up earlier differences) and with them went to war against Turkey to gain Macedonia. These were the Balkan wars of 1912–13. In the first campaigns the allies were quickly successful. Turkey was forced to cede Macedonia; but the allies fell out over its division. Bulgaria launched an unsuccessful attack against Greek and Serbian troops. In the final division of the territory Serbia gained a large part of Macedonia. She immediately began to incorporate it into her state, calling it southern Serbia.

Bosnia-Hercegovina remained the outstanding problem. Unofficially Serbia did everything possible to exacerbate existing hatred of Austrian rule. Tension was increased by Austria's fears over the increase in national movements amongst her many Slav minorities (Czech, Slovak and Polish, and the South Slavs in Hungary, Croatia, Dalmatia and Bosnia-Hercegovina) who looked to Serbia to help in their liberation. Serbian success in the Balkan wars alarmed Austria and decisions were taken that as soon as opportunity arose Serbian power must be destroyed. The opportunity came in 1914 when the Austrian Archduke Franz Ferdinand was murdered in Sarajevo by a Bosnian patriot, Gavrilo Princip. It was not difficult to prove that the arms of Princip and his accomplices had been supplied by a secret Serbian nationalist society, Ujedinjenje ili Smrt – 'unity or death', more commonly known as the Black Hand.

Austria sent Serbia a harsh ultimatum which, to avert a war, Serbian politicians accepted. But Austria had decided this was the

37

time to destroy finally Serbian independence. The Austrian army invaded Serbia on 28 July 1914 and the First World War began.

CROATIA

Croatia-Slavonia and Dalmatia are today joined together in the republic of Croatia, second largest (21,830 square miles) of the republics that make up the federal state of Yugoslavia. Although its three regions had different histories they were often in the past considered as one region and called the Triune Kingdom. Croats form the majority of the population in all parts of the region, and their history has been very different from that of the Serbs. Living nearer to central Europe and the Adriatic Sea, they have been more subject to influence from north and west; they accepted the religion of the Catholic Church of Rome to the exclusion of the Orthodox Church of Constantinople and they participated fully in the cultural heritage of western Europe. This can be seen today in the churches and towns of Croatia – the Gothic cathedral and central European style of houses in the old part of Zagreb for instance, or the many Italian-styled buildings of the Dalmatian coast.

In medieval times Croat lands were in two areas – Pannonian Croatia inland in the north and Dalmatian Croatia which occupied not only northern Dalmatia, but the adjacent parts of Bosnia and Croatia, the greater part of what had been the Roman province of Illyria. Neither region had effective geographical protection and both were frequently invaded from land and sea. Until its final decline in the twelfth century Byzantium claimed suzerainty over Croatia; this was contested in the ninth century by the Franks (who left a permanent memento of themselves in the name of the hills north of Belgrade, the Fruška Gora); other enemies were the Bulgarians (under the Czar Symeon), the Normans of Sicily, and the Tartars. But the two most formidable opponents of the Croats were the Magyars from Hungary in the north, and the Venetians who aimed to control the towns, islands and trade of the Croatian Adriatic coast.

In earliest years before the evolution of their state, the Croats (like the Serbs) lived in tribal and family groups (often in zadrugas), occupying districts known as *župe*. The Croatian state developed out of the concentration of these župe into the hands of a few families who accepted one of their number as king. An independent kingdom of Croatia existed only for a short time, from 910 to 1102. Out- standing kings during that period were Tomislav (910–28), Stephen Držislav (969–95), and Peter Krešimir (1058–74).

The reform of the Catholic Church in the west in the twelfth century had important results in Croatia. After its schism from the eastern Orthodox Church in 1054, the Catholic Church triumphed in Croatia and began a long struggle to eradicate the Croatian custom of celebrating the Catholic liturgy in the Slavonic tongue instead of in Latin. Though repeatedly condemned by the Catholic Church, this was never entirely stamped out; the Slavonic tongue is still used in some Catholic churches in Dalmatia today.

In the eleventh century, the Catholic Church was closely associated with the monarchy in ruling Croatia. A feudal organization of the state developed; churches, monasteries and bishops acquired extensive lands and privileges. At the end of the eleventh century the last native ruler of Croatia died without issue. In 1102 representatives of Croat noble families reached an agreement (known as the Pacta Conventa) with the Hungarian king that he should become king of Croatia but that the Croatian people should retain their independent privileges and customs. Union between Croatia and Hungary lasted until 1918. One of the most remarkable facts of Croatian history after union with Hungary, was that the Croats retained so tenaciously their national consciousness and characteristics.

Feudalism in Croatia developed along lines similar to that in Hungary. Land came to be considered as granted by the king to individual nobles. Land which had belonged to Croats as heads of tribes or clans, now became their individual holdings, thus estates tended to be large and the powers of the nobles greatly increased. In addition, Hungarian nobles were given large estates, especially in Slavonia. Many nobles managed to get exemption from taxation the brunt of which (with disastrous results) came to be borne by the peasants.

The Tartar invasion of Croatia (1241–2), of short duration but causing much destruction, forced the kings to give further powers to any nobles who would fortify castles and be prepared to defend their lands against invasion. It also led to the creation of royal free cities, amongst them Gradec from which the city of Zagreb, present-day capital of Croatia, developed. In one famous district of Turopolje all peasants were given rights of nobility which they retained into modern times.

The most independent and powerful Croatian noble families were the Frankopani (Princes of Krk), the Babonici (with land in Carniola and on the rivers Vrbas, Kupa and Sana), and the Šubici (Princes of Bribir, later known as the Zrinski family). Many of these princes had great influence at the Hungarian court and relics of their power can still be seen in the ruins of magnificent castles in many parts of Croatia.

The situation in Croatia-Slavonia was drastically changed for an interval with the success of the Turkish invasions of the sixteenth century. The Turks defeated the Hungarians at the Battle of Mohacs (1526) and then occupied the greater part of Hungary and Croatia. In the same year the Croats had accepted the Habsburgs as rulers of Croatia, a position they maintained until 1918. Only a few powerful Croatian families survived the Turkish conquest, and their power was eventually liquidated. In the seventeenth century a Croat rebellion against the oppressive policy of the Habsburgs was crushed; the last great Croatian princes, Peter Zrinski and his brother-in-law Krsto Frankopan (who had called in Turkish aid) were executed in 1671 and their lands confiscated.

When the Turks left the Hungarian Croatian lands after the Treaty of Karlovci in 1699, both Austrian and Hungarian powers were increased in Croatia-Slavonia. Austrian and Magyar nobles rather than Croats were settled on land the Turks abandoned, and the military frontier set up in 1578 for defence against the Turks, remained under direct rule of Austria and was later settled by Serbs.

After the end of the seventeenth century, the needs and demands of the feudal nobility were intensified. Population was increasing, there were more consumer goods and a money economy was becoming widespread. The peasants, nearly all of whom had become serfs (except in the Military Frontier) were forced to bear the burden, both of the demands of the nobility and of all taxes exacted by the state. Poverty, lack of privilege and injustice resulted in repeated revolts of peasants, and at times also in the towns where the rigid organization of guilds and the oppressions of town aristocracy also produced large groups of underprivileged people.

The most outstanding rebellion, both for its initial success and for the savagery with which it was suppressed was that under the leadership of Matija Gubec in 1573. This rebellion which received widespread support in north-west Croatia (and in neighbouring Slovene lands) aimed to get back 'old rights' for the peasants, to abolish, the increased obligations and burdens of serfdom; a more extreme demand was for payment of taxes and military service by all classes. These revolutionary demands roused the ruling classes to fury and in crushing the rebellion at least 6,000 peasants were put to death and thousands of villages burnt. Matija Gubec was executed after unspeakable tortures including being crowned with a circlet of red-hot iron in the square in front of St Mark's Church in Zagreb. His name and legend became the inspiration for all future peasant movements against the nobility in Croatia. His fate did not prevent further rebellions in 1651, 1654, 1755, among many others.

The obsolete feudal system prevented modernization and development of the relatively fertile lands of Croatia-Slavonia. From the point of view of their productive capacity many of these lands were underpopulated. The owners of estates, needing as much labour as they could force from the peasants, were desperate to tie labour to the soil to prevent workers from moving into the new industries (mining, timber, boat-building, some food and consumer industries) that began to be developed in Croatia from the eighteenth century onwards.

The 1848 revolutions in the Austro-Hungarian Empire at last gave the opportunity for serfdom to be abolished and the serfs of Croatia became owners of the land they occupied. Property of feudal lords and of the Church became subject to taxation. One result of the abolition of serfdom was the introduction in 1853 of a Civil Code which allowed peasants of Croatia-Slavonia to dissolve the zadrugas in which land had been held communally. In some cases this meant that so many peasants claimed a share of the land that their resulting private holdings were minuscule. A law of 1889 prohibited their further division if resulting farms would be below a minimum of 3–6 yokes.[6] Some zadrugas were not divided and the institution remained in being down to our own times.

Problems of peasant poverty were not solved with the abolition of serfdom. Many of the serfs' holdings were very small (mostly in scattered strips) and most peasants lacked the capital, education and resources to develop them.

Political developments were also important during the nineteenth century. Following the French Revolution and Napoleon's invasion of Europe (which affected Dalmatia more directly than Croatia-Slavonia), ideas of national revival and even liberation began to spread amongst Croats as they did among the other subject peoples of the Austrian Empire. After 1830 Ljudevit Gaj and Count Janko Drašković led a movement for Croat national independence known as the Illyrian movement; one of its aims was the unification of all South Slavs living in lands which had once been the province of Illyria. This movement had little support amongst Croatian peasants, pre-occupied as they were with more immediate economic problems. It gained its greatest support from the comparatively small class of *bourgeois* intellectuals in Zagreb and other Croatian towns and from some nobles and clergy.

The 1848 revolutions in the Habsburg Empire had important repercussions in Croatia. The Magyars of Hungary were themselves in revolt against Austrian Habsburg rule; they aimed to gain greater independence for Hungary. But their leader Louis Kossuth was not willing to make common cause with Croat nationalists, for he intended that Hungary should continue to rule Croatia. His aim was that Magyars should have autonomy, but not Croats, and this was the view of most Magyar leaders. The Hungarian revolt failed. A Croat, Count Jellačić, led Croatian troops to help the Austrian government suppress the Magyar rebels; but this brought little advantage to Croatia. Austria needed Magyar support to maintain her position as a great power. To gain this after the revolt had been crushed, Croatian independence was sacrificed as a gesture of appeasement to Hungary.

A settlement made between Austria and Hungary in 1867 allowed Hungary to dictate her own terms of agreement with Croatia. These terms fell far short of Croat expectations; Croatia was granted limited independence, with autonomy in matters of internal administration, justice, education and ecclesiastical affairs, and the use of the Croatian language on its territory. Croatia was not allowed to incorporate Dalmatia, nor the port of Rijeka (much needed for economic development) and was not given financial independence. The Military Frontier, which included large tracts of Croatian territory, remained under Austria. Croatian aspirations for independence and unity of territories occupied by Croats, thus remained thwarted until the end of the First World War.

The Illyrian (or nationalist) party continued to try to gain national advantages for the Croats under the difficult conditions of the ensuing years. Outstanding names of leaders of the Illyrian party in these years were the Catholic Bishop Strossmeyer (believer in South Slav unity and agreement between Catholic and Orthodox Slavs, friend of Gladstone whose influence he tried to enlist in the South Slav cause), and Ivan Mažuranić, commoner and poet, Ban of Croatia (1870–80) who did much to develop an educational system (a university had been started in Zagreb in 1870). But the party had lost its early *élan* and was divided into factions. Its championship of Croat nationalism was for a time taken over by the Party of Rights under the leadership of Ante Starčević. In later years under Starčević's successors, this party was to become violently chauvinistic and developed into the Ustaše movement, a Croat brand of fascism which was involved in the murder of the first king of Yugoslavia and was responsible for ghastly atrocities and terrorism in Croatia during the Second World War.

After 1867 the Croatian people were faced with many political and economic difficulties. Uppermost was the problem of how far to cooperate with the Hungarian government, whose reaction to increased Croat nationalism was a policy of suppression and Magyarization. On the economic side, the end of the nineteenth and beginning of the twentieth century was a period of instability, with frequent bad harvests and agrarian crises. The Hungarian government did little to help, for it was not willing to see a prosperous Croatia. Many emigrated during this period. Most of the Croats (total population of about 2·5 million in 1906) were peasants living on small holdings; after long centuries of feudalism they were more politically passive than the peasants of Serbia, but like them they hated the government and were contemptuous of the townspeople, even those who were Croats like themselves.

There was some limited industrial development and urban population was increasing. This helped the evolution of new political ideas and new leaders. The Social Democrat Party was founded in 1895 and two new leaders were Frano Supilo and Ante Trumbić. In 1905 two brothers, Antun and Stephen Radić founded the Croat Peasant Party to educate the Croat peasants, represent their interests and mobilize support for a Croat independence movement. This party helped to bring about a coalition between Croats and the Serbs of the Vojvodina. It played an increasingly important part in Croat politics up to the outbreak of war in 1914 and a vital part in the political life of the Kingdom of Yugoslavia.

DALMATIA

Dalmatia is a narrow strip of land on the Adriatic coast of Yugoslavia, running from Istria in the north to the Gulf of Kotor in the south – a distance of about 210 miles – including the thousand or so islands that lie in its coastal waters. At its widest it is never more than 35 miles, and at some points is little over a mile wide, for it does not include the hinterland.

From early history Dalmatia had close historical associations with Croatia; over threequarters of its population was Croat and, as in Croatia, the overwhelming majority of the people were Catholic.

The history of the province (after the Greek and Roman periods) is very complex. In early medieval times parts of Dalmatia were conquered by Byzantium, by Franks, Hungarians and the independent South Slav states of Croatia, Serbia and Bosnia. Later came the Ottoman Turks, but the greatest influence was the Venetians, who ruled over most of Dalmatia from the thirteenth to the eighteenth centuries. Relics of their occupation can be seen today in houses and churches in every part of the coast and its islands. Venetian rule came to an end when Napoleon's army invaded Dalmatia and occupied it from 1806 to 1813. In 1815 Dalmatia was assigned by the Congress of Vienna to Austria, by whom it was ruled until 1918.

In spite of the influx of foreign peoples, the population of Dalmatia remained predominantly Slavonic. We know now that the people of Dubrovnik – both nobles and ordinary citizens – were mainly Slavs for they spoke Serbo-Croat in their homes even though they used Latin as their legal, and Italian as their trading languages. This was probably true of many other towns of the coastland.[7] The Slavonic population was continually strengthened by waves of refugees after each invasion of the interior, and especially during periods of Turkish oppression in Croatia and Serbia.

One group of refugees were the Uskoks who built themselves an almost impregnable fortress at Senj. They became expert sailors and pirates and preyed on trading ships of the Adriatic for over a hundred years, gaining an almost legendary reputation, until they were eventually defeated by the Austrians and deported to the interior of Croatia in the eighteenth century.

Special mention must also be made of the republic of Dubrovnik which had a unique history until its incorporation into the Austrian province of Dalmatia in 1815. In the medieval period Dubrovnik acknowledged the suzerainty of Venice and even accepted until 1356 a Venetian count as nominal head of government. Thereafter Dubrovnik was a wealthy independent city state ruled by a small group of about a dozen noble families. It became rich through trade – just how rich can be seen from the magnificent buildings in the city today. In the Middle Ages, its merchants went to Constantinople to fetch spices and luxury goods that came from further east. They also had widespread trading activities in Italy and in the interior of the Balkans; in Bosnia and Serbia they had a special position buying not only agricultural produce but exploiting the mines and exporting gold, silver, copper and lead.

Although the townspeople were much more numerous in Dalmatia

than they were in Croatia and Serbia, a large, ultimately predominant peasant population cultivated the land outside the towns. When
Venice obtained supremacy over the coast it imposed its own system
of government and landholding. Serfdom (known as *kmetsvo*) was
eventually abolished in 1878 but the colonate system was continued
after Austria took over the area from Venice, and it remained in
being even after 1918.

The land of Dalmatia is infertile. In some parts grain and vegetables could be grown, but the greater part of the area was under
vine and olive cultivation. 'The country abounds everywhere with
the olive and vine' wrote the Greek geographer Strabo about A.D.
17, adding that much of the land was 'sterile, unsuited to agriculture
and barely affording subsistence to the inhabitants'. The same
description continued to be given by travellers down the ages.[8]
Poverty of the peasants is noted by all and was still one of the
characteristics which made a deep impression on Dame Rebecca
West when she visited Dalmatia shortly before the outbreak of the
Second World War.[9]

The Venetians strove to keep Dalmatia poor lest it compete with
their already dwindling trade. They even forbade education of Slav
people in their own language. They used only Italian as the language
of administration, and inhabitants of Dalmatia had to become
bilingual, Italian and Serbo-Croat, a habit which persisted until
our own times. Though the Austrians after 1815 introduced some
economic improvements, and allowed the Slavs to be educated and
governed in their own language, economic conditions in Dalmatia
did not greatly improve during their administration. The people of
Dalmatia had to wait until the second half of the twentieth
century before they got the industries and development to abolish
their hitherto chronic poverty.

SLOVENIA

Slovenia, which lies in the Alpine mountains and foothills in the
north of Yugoslavia has had no spectacular history as a province and
never became an independent medieval state. Today, Slovenia, one of
the smallest of the republics in Yugoslavia, with an area of 7,819

square miles and a population of 1,462,961, comprises the former Austrian crownland of Carniola, a large part of Istria and Styria, a small part of Carinthia and parts of Gorizia and Gradisca. This is much less than the territory originally inhabited by Slovenes when they first settled in the region in the sixth century. By the eighth century German rulers had encroached on Slovene lands so success, fully that they were accepted as rulers throughout the medieval period. In the sixteenth century Carniola became an Austrian crown, land, a possession of the House of Habsburg, and the Slovene people of this and the surrounding areas remained within the Austrian Empire until 1918.

Like the Austrians and Germans, the Slovenes became Catholic and like them (but unique amongst the South Slavs) they came under the influence of the reformation. A great name in Slovene history is that of Primož Trubar (1508–86) a religious and social reformer whose ideas obtained a large peasant following. But the Slovenes with the other people of the Habsburg dominions were subjected to the full weight of the counter-reformation, and Protestantism was virtually eradicated in Slovenia; the Catholic Church came to play (until the Second World War) a very important part in political and social life.

Yet in spite of long years of Germanization, the Slovenes retained very strongly their national identity. Their language (forbidden as a language of education and public administration until after 1848) remained Slovene, written in Latin characters and akin to the Serbo-Croat language of most of the other South Slavs. Until very recently all Slovenes were brought up to be bi-lingual in German and Slovene. A Slovene literary tradition was maintained and flourished in the nineteenth century under the influence of Prešeren, Levstik and other writers. In art, the Slovenes also developed their own, especially peasant traditions to be seen in costumes, woodcraft, the decorations of their homes, implements – even beehives – and also in the decoration of some of their parish churches. The larger churches and castles (of which Slovenia has very many) and the buildings in the towns were influenced by the palladian and baroque styles of Austria and south Germany. Examples of these can be seen in churches (the

Ursuline and Franciscan churches in Ljubljana), houses (in Ljubljana and Maribor for instance), and castles (of Ptuj, Žužemberg and Bled among many others); examples of folk art can be seen in villages and the many local museums of Slovenia today.

Though Austrian rule limited Slovene national development, it brought some marked benefits. The Turks never conquered Slovenia (though they made a number of raids) and its lands were thus saved from the devastation of their occupation suffered in Serbia and parts of Croatia. There were no great migrations into Slovene lands, no large-scale resettlement as among the other South Slavs, with the result that the Slovenes remained a homogeneous national group living on the same territory throughout the centuries. As most of the land is mountainous, much of it poor and unfertile, this, like mountain regions in other South Slav lands, became overpopulated. There was much rural poverty, even starvation, and in the decades before the First World War many Slovenes emigrated.

In modern times peasants came to supplement their income by work in forestry or minor industries. Domestic industries were developed in all regions of Slovenia, often with specialities (lace, weaving, basketwork, woodwork)[10] for different regions. Home industries were gradually superseded by factories and mining; metallurgy and textiles drew off the surplus peasant population, but wages were low and there was still considerable rural poverty in Slovenia until the twentieth century.

In the nineteenth century improved farming, aided by credits and the sale of agricultural surpluses, was encouraged by the development of agricultural co-operatives. These organizations were assisted by the Catholic Slovene People's Party and by the fact that alone among the South Slav peasants at this time, almost all Slovenes were educated. Though conservative and strongly attached to their land, they were sufficiently educated to take advantage of the agricultural and industrial as well as political changes of the age.

The tenacity of the Slovene people is shown by the fact that they preserved their own language during centuries of Austrian rule. Latent nationalism was further developed when Napoleon incorporated Slovenia into his province of Illyria, of which Ljubljana (main town of Slovenia today) became the capital. Although Germanization was resumed when Slovenia was restored to Austria in 1815, Slovene nationalism continued to grow and found expression in many cultural, economic and sports (*sokol*) organizations during the nineteenth and early twentieth centuries. Thus when the unity of the South Slavs began to be discussed before and during the First World War, the Slovenes were able to produce effective leaders and were ready to play their part in the creation of the new state of Yugoslavia.

BOSNIA-HERCEGOVINA

Although Bosnia-Hercegovina was another province that came to be ruled by Austria, it had a very different history from that of Slovenia. Like other South Slav provinces, its history was greatly influenced by geographical position and the inaccessible character of its forested mountains. Lying between Serbia to the east and south, Croatia to the north and west, and being the hinterland to the Adriatic coast, it was subjected to many conflicting influences. Wars and migrations resulted in a mixture of Serbs and Croats populating the region. Both Catholic and Orthodox Churches attempted to win the people to their unique authority. Throughout the Middle Ages and up to the Turkish conquest in 1463, Bogomilism had many followers in Bosnia, who resisted repeated attempts – even powerful crusades – to convert or extirpate them.[11]

It is difficult to tell from the Greek and Catholic sources which comprise most of the material about Bogomils in Bosnia, how far the majority of its supporters accepted the stark ascetic beliefs and dualism that stemmed from the Manichees, and how far support was based on a desire for a national Bosnian Church that would be free from political pressures from Rome and Constantinople, and had its roots in an earlier Christianization of the region during the Roman period.

Bosnia first became an effective independent state under its famous ruler Kulin (1180-1203) himself a supporter of an independent Bosnian Church and accused of being a Bogomil. Though Bosnia continued to be more or less independent for over 150 years, it was never a strong unified state with a powerful central authority. It was a feudal state in which Churches and nobility owned large estates and peasants held land under feudal obligations, similar to those in medieval Serbia and Croatia. The wild, inaccessible nature of Bosnia's mountainous lands made it possible for nobles to be virtually kings in their own territory. Foreign invasions (from Serbia under Dušan and repeatedly from Hungary and Croatia) encouraged nobles to oppose the creation of a centralized government, resulting in long periods of civil war. This prevented the economic development of the country – in spite of the existence of valuable silver mines (at Srebrenica) and the trading activities of Dubrovnik merchants. The position of peasants deteriorated and by the end of the Middle Ages there were few free peasants left in Bosnia.

When the Turks first began to invade at the end of the fourteenth century, they were welcomed by many Bosnians. Many members of the Bosnian Church converted to Islam (they had for centuries been persecuted by the Catholic, and to a less extent the Orthodox, Churches) and the nobles in particular accepted the Mohammedan religion as a means of keeping their estates.

Feudal serfs who converted to Islam became free peasants. Christians who did not convert, and of whatever class, became serfs – the rayah, who like those in Serbia and the rest of the Turkish empire, had no rights of property or citizenship under Moslem law. In Serbia the Christian communities, though under Turkish rule, were in the majority and allowed to retain some kind of local and social independence. In Bosnia and Hercegovina Christians were crushed and exploited both by Turks who became landowners and by their own converted upper classes.

The Turks had to fight a number of campaigns before Bosnia and Hercegovina were finally conquered in 1463 and 1482 and by that time the ruling family and nobles were virtually liquidated. Bosnia and Hercegovina became a Turkish province (ruled from Jajce, not Sarajevo which became the main town of the province only later) and eventually became a stronghold of the most conservative type of Mohammedanism.

Turkey introduced its own feudal system into Bosnia (similar to that described for Serbia above) and as the Turkish empire receded during the seventeenth and eighteenth centuries, many Turks – officials and janissaries – came to acquire estates in this province. During these years the Turkish feudal system deteriorated; feudal dues and labour service were often illegally increased. Taxes were raised and savagely enforced; owners of large estates demanded exemption from taxation. It was the aggravation of these conditions that led to repeated peasant revolts in Bosnia and Hercegovina in the nineteenth century. In Turkey itself, a *tanzimat*, or programme of reforms, was instituted in 1826 and reforming edicts were issued in 1839, 1856, 1864 and 1876. But Bosnia was a long way from Constantinople and the Turkish central government was powerless to enforce its reforms in so distant a province against the wishes of both landed class and many of the officials.

The most serious revolt – and one of far-reaching consequences – was that which broke out in Hercegovina in 1874 and spread to Bosnia. The conditions which caused the revolt were beginning to be well known to the outside world. Most of the great powers had had consuls and representatives in Bosnia since the middle of the century. Bosnia and Hercegovina had also been visited by many nineteenth-century travellers to the Balkans who found the Turkish provinces both attractive and repellent because of the savage grandeur of their landscape and the savage brutality of their rule. Among these were Miss Irby, an Englishwoman, who travelled through Bosnia in 1875 and set up her own school in Sarajevo for the training of women teachers (her exploits were subsequently honoured by naming a street of that town after her), and Sir Arthur Evans who also explored Bosnia on foot in the same year.[12]

It is not surprising that it was generally believed in Europe that Turkey would lose these provinces. But by 1875 the solution of the Bosnian question was already bound up with nineteenth-century power politics.

South Slav nationalism was already well developed in the Balkans by this time; Serbia was eager to include Bosnia-Hercegovina within her small new state and had the powerful argument that 43 per cent of Bosnians were Orthodox Serbs, another 18 per cent Catholic

Croats, and many of the remaining 39 per cent Moslems were of South Slav race. But Serbia was still too weak to enforce her claims without Russian aid, and Russia had decided that Serbian rule over Bosnia-Hercegovina would not help to advance her own aims.

Having failed to make a negotiated settlement, Russia fought Turkey in 1877 and though she won the war, she lost the peace which was signed at Berlin in 1878.

To the Bosnian people who had hoped that the war would bring them some kind of freedom the treaty of Berlin which assigned their country to Austria was a bitter disappointment. Although Austrian rule (occupation was changed to annexation by Austria in 1908) brought many changes and some improvements, little was done to solve the agrarian problems which had been the major source of discontent. The Austrian government did not change the existing land-tenure system. Some 7,000 Moslem landowners (about 0·5 per cent of the total population) had large estates on which were settled about 85,000 families of feudal serfs (both Christian and Moslem) tied to the land for which they had to pay excessive proportions (usually an eighth) of its produce in addition to labour service.[13] Such conditions had been abolished with serfdom in the rest of the Austrian empire in 1848, but they remained in being in Bosnia until the empire itself was abolished in 1918.

Without land reform, attempts to modernize agriculture were useless. Conditions of peasant life remained miserable and a source of permanent enmity between the peasants and the landlords as well as against the Austrian rulers who had taken over the land and done so little to solve its worst problem.

What Austria did introduce was greater security and a more efficient system of administration as well as some industrial development. Road and railways were built linking the main towns of the interior with Austrian lands. Forestry resources were exploited and mines unworked for many years were reopened.[14] Yet these improvements did not ease tension and dissatisfaction caused by alien rule and agrarian poverty. The movement for freedom for the South Slav people of Bosnia and Hercegovina gained increased support within the province and more, if clandestine, help from the neighbouring kingdom of Serbia. This was the situation that led to the murder of the Austrian Archduke Franz Ferdinand by a Bosnian youth in Sarajevo in June 1914.

In Sarajevo today, the place where Princip stood when he fired on the Archduke is marked by the imprint (recently made) of his boots on the concrete pavement. The near-by bridge over the river Miljačka is called Princip's Bridge, and his name and those of his accomplices in a nationalist organization, are today honoured as martyrs in the fight for Bosnia's independence, won as a result of the world war which followed the Archduke's murder.

MONTENEGRO

Shut away high up in the mountains of the Dinaric range, inland from the southern Adriatic coast, Montenegro was able to be more independent than any other region inhabited by the South Slavs. The rocky peaks and high plateaux lay away from the main lines of communication through the Balkans; access was difficult both from the Adriatic coast and the interior and the land was too infertile to be much temptation to invaders. For centuries the Montenegrins were left to develop their own forms of government and society, which remained primitive and undeveloped down to the twentieth century.

In early times Montenegro (called Duklja or Dioclea) was governed by its own powerful families. Later, in the time of the Nemanjić kings, it came under the rule of Serbia. It had contacts with Croatia as well as Serbia and received Christianity from both Catholic and Orthodox Churches. Eventually, like Serbia, it became predominantly Orthodox, and in time came to adopt the Cyrillic (not the Latin as in Croatia and Slovenia) alphabet for its written language.

After the disintegration of the Serbian state in the fourteenth century, the people of this region (known for a time as Zeta) were left to their own resources. They fought with both Croats and Serbs against the Turks who made repeated attempts to invade and subdue the lands of the black mountains – Crnagora or Montenegro as it finally came to be called. Though the Turks were able to conquer the foothills and impose tribute (a ducat for each family and a round sum of 1,000 ducats per annum), they were never able effectively to occupy the mountains.

Nominally Montenegro remained under Turkey until the seventeenth century. Some of her leading families ruled and collected taxes for the Turks and were converted to Islam, though they were later forcibly reconverted to Christianity. The country was never successfully subdued, and fighting the Turks became a permanent occupation of Montenegrin men. 'So predominant is the idea of the soldier over that of the citizen', wrote a traveller, A. A. Paton, in 1849, 'that even when a child is baptised, pistols are put in the infant's mouth to kiss, and then laid in the cradle beside him; and one of the favourite toasts drunk on the occasion is "May he never die in his bed".'[15]

The Orthodox Metropolitan Bishop of Montenegro, the Vladika, was the military as well as the spiritual leader of his people. At the end of the seventeenth century Daniele Petrović-Njegoš was elected Vladika and for over a hundred and fifty years his family ruled Montenegro as Prince Bishops. The most famous was Vladika Rade Peter Petrović Njegoš II (1830–51), an enlightened ruler who tried to modernize his country and educate its people. He was a poet whose best known epic poem *The Mountain-Wreath* is still claimed as outstanding in Yugoslav literature.[16]

In spite of Peter II's efforts, Montenegro still remained backward and primitive with only a rudimentary state organization. The offices of prince and bishop were separated in 1851, and in 1878 (after successful campaigns against the Turks) the territory of Montenegro was enlarged by almost three-quarters, its population more than doubled and recognized as an independent princedom. Prince Nicholas ruled from 1860 to 1918 when Montenegro was incorporated into the new state of Yugoslavia; he took the title of King in 1910. Montenegro also obtained additional territory from Turkish lands in Macedonia and the Sanjak of Novi Pazar in 1913 after the Balkan wars in which she fought with Serbia and Bulgaria against Turkey. Today, in the federal republic of Yugoslavia Montenegro (5,342 square miles and 419,625 population) is one of the smallest of the autonomous republics. It at last has Adriatic coastlands including the great sea inlet of the Boka Kotorska and the little ancient port of Budva.

Social and political life was organized on a patriarchal tribal system, in which family ties, the *bratsvo*, were all important. Relationships in the bratsvo[17] and tribe were governed by many archaic and barbarous customs. The most deep-rooted and socially destructive of these was the blood feud which demanded that insult, injury or death caused to a member of a bratsvo should be wiped out in blood. The system was self-perpetuating. Milovan Djilas has described the havoc and perpetual fighting that this custom wreaked on his own Montenegrin family:

> My father's grandfather, my own two grandfathers, my father and my uncle were killed, as though a dread curse lay on them. My father and his brother and my brothers were killed even though all of them yearned to die peacefully in their beds beside their wives. Generation after generation, and the bloody chain was not broken. The inherited fear and hatred of feuding clans was stronger than fear and hatred of the enemy, the Turks.[18]

An attempt was made in the nineteenth century to impose more civilized forms of government with a legal code and systems of justice and taxation. But enforcement was a difficult task; government remained essentially patriarchal. The customs of the bratsvo and blood feud still continued and only began to be eradicated after the end of the Second World War.

The heavy losses of manpower from these feuds and from perpetual guerrilla warfare against the Turks left Montenegro very weak; natural resources were poor, and the climate and country very harsh. Animal husbandry was the common occupation (carried on mostly by women, old people and children). There were few large estates and the forests and mountain pastures were held in common or belonged to a bratsvo. Arable lands and larger estates were included in the territory Montenegro acquired in 1878 and 1913 and for these Turkey had to be indemnified. The land still remained overpopulated for its productive capacity, and there was large-scale emigration. Trade was very simple – livestock on the hoof, dried meat, hides, wool, honey and wax were exported, textiles, salt, coffee and sugar were imported. The equally important import of guns and gun-powder was largely paid for by the annual subsidy which Montenegro received from Russia.

Montenegro's connection with Russia had begun as far back as the reign of Peter the Great, Czar of Russia, who requested aid from Montenegro when he was at war with Turkey in 1710. Close relations were maintained (both countries belonged to the Orthodox Church) and Montenegro remained a pensioner of Russia until the end of its existence as an independent state. Many Montenegrins were opposed to the incorporation of their country in a Yugoslav state in 1918, and the new government had to be enforced on the people before they were prepared to give up either their anarchic indepen-dence or their archaic customs.[19]

MACEDONIA

In the south of the Balkans is the territory of Macedonia which today is divided between Yugoslavia, Bulgaria and Greece. This region lies between the Šar mountains on the west, the Rhodope mountains on the east and the Aegean sea with the port of Salonica to the south; in the north is Serbia. Two important rivers, the Vardar and the Struma (each with many tributaries), run from north to south of the region to outlets in the Aegean Sea, and in the south-west corner are two great lakes, Prespa and Ohrid. It is a land of high mountains and well-watered plains; of mediterranean climate and mixed agri-culture. In the mountains nomadic Vlachs still move their flocks of sheep to high pastures in the summer. The foothills and the valleys produce grain, vegetables and fruit; there are poultry and cattle, in-cluding water-buffalo, and because of its hot climate the region produces such special crops as poppies (for opium), tobacco and flax. The people of the region are as diverse as their crops, for Macedonia is inhabited by Albanians, Greeks, Turks, Jews, gypsies and Vlachs, in addition to the majority population, the Macedonian Slavs.

Because of its strategic position and ease of access from the Aegean Sea via the Vardar and Struma Valleys, Macedonia has been fought over and occupied by many different peoples. It was occupied by Greeks, Romans and Byzantines. All built towns and had busy trade-routes running north to the Danube and central Europe, and west to the Adriatic. Slavonic tribes settled the region in the sixth century, became subjects of the Byzantine Empire and later received Christianity from Constantinople accepting the authority of the Greek Orthodox patriarch. At the end of the ninth century most of Macedonia was conquered by the first Bulgarian Empire under Czar Symeon (893–927). Later a Macedonian Emperor Samuel (976–1014) ruled both Macedonia and Bulgaria from his capital at Prespa. After Samuel's death, his empire disintegrated and Macedonia was controlled by various Byzantine rulers until part of it was conquered by King Milutin Nemanja of Serbia in the fourteenth century. The Serbian Emperor Dušan conquered the greater part of Macedonia and made his capital at Skopje where he was crowned emperor and issued his famous code of laws. Thus history gave the basis for Serbs, Bulgarians and Greeks to make claims to Macedonian lands.

After the death of Dušan in 1355, Macedonia was conquered by the Turks and part of it remained a Turkish province until the twentieth century; some of its Slavonic inhabitants were converted to Islam. By the nineteenth century the strategic importance of Macedonia had made it a bone of contention between the great powers. Russia wished to control the region because of its propinquity to Constantinople and the straits which allow entrance to the Black Sea. She had an excuse for intervention because of notorious Turkish misrule of the province and because a large number of its Slavonic people belonged to the Orthodox Church. Austria, as has been shown above, wished to expand through the Balkans and control the port of Salonica. The small independent state of Serbia claimed Macedonia because its inhabitants were Orthodox Slavs and aimed to incorporate it within her frontiers.

In 1870 the Turkish government, perhaps to augment existing discord, allowed the Bulgarians to establish an independent Orthodox Church (the Exarchate) with authority in most of Macedonia. The Bulgarians used the Church to spread their political and cultural influence throughout the province. Although the Serbs tried to counter this, they were at a disadvantage as they had no official standing in Macedonia. Strife between the two peoples for influence over the Macedonians continued into the twentieth century. A further complicating factor was introduced after 1877–8 when Russia defeated Turkey and in the abortive Treaty of San Stefano, proposed the creation of a great Bulgarian state which would have stretched from the Black Sea to Albania and the Aegean.

As has been shown above, this proposed settlement was superseded by the Treaty of Berlin which created a very much smaller independent state of Bulgaria, and put most of Macedonia back under Turkish rule. This was a great disappointment to Macedonians who had hoped to get some form of autonomy. It was bitterly resented by Bulgarians whose appetite for a large state had been whetted by the proposals of San Stefano, and it left the Serbs determined to take the first opportunity to win Macedonia both from Turkey and from their Bulgarian rivals.

The disappointments of the whole Balkan settlement of the Berlin Treaty led eventually to the Balkan wars of 1912–13 in which Serbia, Bulgaria and Greece first allied together to wrest Macedonia from Turkey; when that had been successfully accomplished, the victors quarrelled as to how the territory should be divided between them. Bulgaria attacked her allies and was defeated by them with the result that by the Treaty of Bucharest in 1913 Greece received southern Macedonia including Salonica, Bulgaria was assigned a small part of eastern Macedonia, and Serbia received a great part of the Vardar valley including Skopje (the Turkish Uskub), Bitolj (Monastir), and western Macedonia with the greater part of lakes Ohrid and Prespa. Although Serbian (later Yugoslav) Macedonia was attacked and occupied by Bulgaria in both world wars, the peace treaties reassigned these parts of Macedonia to Yugoslavia.

What was the attitude of the Macedonian people during these years of political strife over their province? During the last years of Turkish occupation there were many unsuccessful revolts against excessive taxation and harsh rule; that which started in 1903 on Ilinden (2 August, Elijah's day) was one of the most serious. In 1893 a Macedonian liberation movement was founded which developed into the famous Internal Macedonian Revolutionary Organization (IMRO) led by two Macedonian nationalists Damian Gruev and Goce Delčev. Today they are claimed as heroes by all Macedonians. From early days this movement was split between those who favoured an autonomous Macedonia and those who (financed and supported by the Bulgarian Foreign Office) aimed to incorporate all Macedonia into Bulgaria. This latter move/ ment organized terrorist activities in Macedonia until it became so out of hand that it had to be suppressed by the Bulgarian govern/ ment in 1929. Though many Macedonians were forced to take part in these struggles the major interest of most inhabitants of the province was in preserving their homes and livelihood.[20]

Turkish rule in Macedonia (which lasted for 530 years) was based on the same system as that in other parts of the Balkans. Macedonia was of special importance to the Turks as it controlled the strategic economic highway between the port of Salonica and Europe. Thus the towns were heavily occupied by Turkish soldiers, and Turkish rule and exactions became more severe as she fought a rearguard action to retain this vital possession.

Macedonia was unique in the fact that some Turkish peasants came as settlers and were given smallholdings of between ten and fifteen hectares (one hectare= 2·471 acres), adding yet another ele/ ment to the mixed population. But the greater part of the land came to be held (often by absentee landlords and managed by tax/farmers) in tenancies called čiftliks. The tenants who worked on the čiftliks, the Christian rayahs, were obliged to deliver to their landlord between one third and one half of their produce and to give him labour service. Thus social injustice added to political disturbance and the infertile character of large parts of the land resulted in poor production and over/population. Many Macedonians emigrated and others sought work abroad for periods of years – these were called pečalbari, temporary emigrants.

The acquisition of Vardar Macedonia by Serbia in 1913 nearly doubled the size of her territory and added over half a million people to her population. In the few months that remained before the out/ break of the First World War Serbia was unable to effect many changes in the province or to enforce on its inhabitants a feeling of Serbian nationalism; nor was it easy in the period between the two wars for Macedonians to feel convinced that they should be Yugoslavs first and Macedonians second. The problems of economic development necessary to raise the inhabitants of Macedonia from debased poverty had to be tackled before they were likely to accept Yugoslav nationalism; these were not solved before the Second World War and were left to be dealt with by the Yugoslav republic after 1945.

Vardar Macedonia, in spite of its chequered and bloody history and in spite of considerable industrial development in the second half of the twentieth century, remains one of the most beautiful in scenery, the richest in historical association of all the republics of presentday Yugoslavia. In spite too of all that can be said about later Turkish misrule, the Moslem policy of religious toleration allowed the beautiful churches and monasteries of Macedonia to escape destruction. Today restored churches such as that of the ancient Patriarchate at Peć, the frescoed churches of St Naum, St Kliment, St Sophia, and others at Ohrid and in other parts of Macedonia, are amongst the most beautiful in the world.

In modern times there have been many disputes about the origins of Macedonian Slavs – are they Serbs or Bulgars, or are they a separate branch of the South Slav Peoples? In the past, Serbia and Bulgaria pushed their claims – with many specious arguments – in the hope of establishing a claim to the whole territory. Noncontroversial opinion usually accepts the view that Macedonians are a separate branch of the South Slavs with close affinities both with the Serbs and Bulgars.

Today the Yugoslav Macedonian Republic, 10,229 square miles and 1,303,906 population, has autonomy and the opportunity to develop its own language and culture. Though not the smallest of the Yugoslav republics, it was until recently (with Montenegro) the poorest. Special federal investments of the past fifteen years have begun to industrialize and develop the rich resources of the region (and to rebuild Skopje after the 1963 earthquake), in the belief that prosperity for Macedonia is long overdue, and that it is the best means of ensuring political stability.

SLOVENIA

14 Ljubljana in Slovenia illustrates the Austrian and German architectural style which predominates in this region as a result of early conquest.

15 The Slovenes developed their own form of art in a predominantly peasant tradition; even beehives were decorated as seen in this panel from a beehive dating from the nineteenth century.

SERBIA

16 This fresco dating from the fourteenth century at the Serbian Orthodox Monastery at Gračanica is one of the many legacies from the Byzantine Empire which had such a strong effect on Serbian history.

17 The last and greatest of the Nemanjić family, who ruled Serbia from the twelfth to the fourteenth centuries, was Stephen Dušan. His Code issued in 1349, a page of which is reproduced here, gives a vivid impression of feudal society in medieval Serbia.

18 In this drawing dating from the early nineteenth century a man is seen playing the gusle. This instrument was used by minstrels who sang heroic ballads bemoaning Serbian defeat by the Turks at Kosovo in 1389.

CROATIA

19 In the eleventh century the Catholic Church triumphed in Croatia, Slavonia and Dalmatia which today form the republic of Croatia. The famous portal of the Cathedral at Šibenik reflects the cultural heritage of Western Christendom.

20 The Venetians ruled Dalmatia from the thirteenth to the eighteenth centuries and their influence is clearly evident at the coastal town of Siran.

21 The ancestors of this typical Croatian farmer struggled under the serfdom inflicted by Turkey and Austria between the sixteenth and nineteenth centuries.

BOSNIA-HERCEGOVINA

22 Jajce once capital of Bosnia-Hercegovina which was a Turkish province in the fifteenth century became an important meeting-place for Marshal Tito and the Partisans during the Second World War.

23 Turkey introduced its own feudal system into Bosnia and heavy taxes were inflicted. In this nineteenth-century drawing a Bosnian rayah pays tribute.

MONTENEGRO

24 These people in the mountain
town of Andrijevica illustrate the
primitive fashion of life in Montenegro which because of its geographical position has remained
isolated from outside influences.

25 The Orthodox Metropolitan
Bishop of Montenegro, the Vladika,
was both military and spiritual
leader of his people. The most
famous was Vladika Rade Peter
Petrović Njegoš II (1830-51). Sculpture by Ivan Meštrović.

MACEDONIA

26–8 The hot climate of Macedonia, a territory with a diverse history, allows for the production of rice (*above*), poppies for opium (*centre*) and tobacco (*below*).

3   The Kingdom of Yugoslavia

FROM THE BEGINNING of the First World War it was clear that the future of all South Slavs was at stake; that the issue between Allies and Central Powers would decide not only whether Serbia should remain independent, but also whether the South Slavs of the Austro-Hungarian Empire should gain their freedom. In 1914, the Serbian parliament declared its aim to be 'the liberation and unification of all our subjugated brothers, Serbs, Croats and Slovenes'.[21]

Austria did not achieve the anticipated easy victory when she invaded Serbia on 28 July 1914. The Serbs, with only 450,000 men (later mobilization totalled 707,000) and short of rifles and ammunition, repulsed the first Austrian attack in the west and north-west. Austria used over half a million men, of whom 273,804 were lost.

Serbian losses were also heavy, and a typhus epidemic in the winter of 1914-15 killed more than the losses in battle. An Allied force landed at Salonica in February 1915, but it was unable to move up the Vardar valley to Serbia's aid. In October 1915 Austria, reinforced by German and Bulgarian support, returned to the attack. By December, the Serbian army was defeated but refused to surrender and the order was given to retreat through Montenegro and Albania to the Adriatic coast, in the hope of being able to re-group and receive Allied help.

They retreated across the high barren mountains of Montenegro and Albania in extreme winter conditions, receiving a hostile reception from the inhabitants who showed little South Slav solidarity. Believing that the Germans would win the war, King Nicholas of

Montenegro fled to France after ordering his people not to aid the retreating Serbs. Thousands of Serbian soldiers and refugees died of exposure and starvation in this retreat before the remaining 155,000 troops reached the coast and were evacuated by the Allies to Corfu. Later, a regrouped Serbian army joined the Allied forces at Salonica and when the break through came at the end of the war, they led the attack up the Vardar and Morava valleys driving the Germans and their allies out of Serbia.

This heroic resistance and eventual success confirmed Serbian leaders in their already strongly held belief that they should be accepted as leaders of the South Slav liberation movement.

During the war the movement for South Slav unity had gathered momentum. On 30 April 1915 in Paris, a Yugoslav Committee was formed by South Slavs from the Austro-Hungarian lands. Among its leading supporters were the Croat sculptor Ivan Meštrović, Ante Trumbić and Frano Supilo. In May the Committee moved to London and continued to work for the support of Allied leaders and of South Slavs all over the world. Two Englishmen, H. Wickham Steed, editor of *The Times*, and R. W. Seton Watson did much to help the Committee to gain support for the Yugoslav cause and to publicize the ethnic and historical background to the South Slav claims. Allied statesmen were clearly ignorant of the situation in the Balkans, for almost at the same time as the Yugoslav Committee was founded, negotiations to persuade Italy to join the Allies had resulted in the Secret Treaty of London (26 April 1915). In return for her entry into the war on the Allied side, Italy was promised Trieste, Gorizia-Gradisca, Istria and part of Dalmatia; with the exception of the city of Trieste, these Austrian lands had a predominantly South Slav population. The terms of this 'secret' treaty were soon known to the Yugoslav Committee, and the indignation they aroused helped South Slavs to realize that they would have to work together if they were to achieve their aims.

The Austro-Hungarian Empire was still in existence, but its disintegration had already begun. Croats, Slovenes and Serbs, conscripted from the Austro-Hungarian lands, refused to fight and thousands gave themselves up to the enemy on the Russian and the

Italian fronts. In May 1917 Slovene deputies in the Austrian parliament passed a resolution demanding autonomy within the empire.
Two months later on 20 July, a declaration signed at Corfu by
representatives of Serbia and the Yugoslav Committee announced
that all Slovenes, Croats and Serbs would join together after the war
to form a united democratic kingdom under the rule of the Karadjordjević dynasty of Serbia. The form this kingdom was to take was
not defined. President Wilson after initial hesitation, came out in
favour of complete independence for the minorities of the Austrian
Empire. Bosnia-Hercegovina and Montenegro decided to join the
Serbs, Croats and Slovenes. On 1 December 1918 the Kingdom of
Serbs, Croats and Slovenes (officially called Yugoslavia after 1929)
came into being, with Alexander, former Regent of Serbia, as
King.

Final decisions about frontiers caused heated disputes at the Peace
Conference.[22] President Wilson refused to endorse all Italy's claims
to South Slav occupied lands, but Italy eventually gained Trieste,
most of Istria, four Adriatic islands, and the city of Zadar (Treaty of
Rapallo, 12 November 1920). Before a decision had been reached
about Fiume, the Italian poet, D'Annunzio occupied Rijeka
(Fiume), and though he was eventually forced to evacuate it, the city
was retained by Italy until the Second World War.

Most of the other frontier problems (except that of the Klagenfurt-
Villach region of Carinthia on the border with Austria) were solved
in Yugoslavia's favour. A small increase of territory at Bulgaria's
expense was added in the east to give a strategic frontier. The acquisition from Hungary of the Vojvodina (including Bačka, Baranja and
the western half of the Banat) brought a mixed population of Serbs,
Magyars, Germans, Rumanians and some Slovaks. Kosovo-
Metohija, an ancient historical province of medieval Serbia, but
largely populated by Albanians, was also included. Other minorities
were Turks and Vlachs in Macedonia, as well as people who considered themselves Bulgarian along the eastern frontier; on the
Adriatic coastland were Italians. The peace treaties incorporated
guarantees to these minority peoples.

The brief record of the events which led to the creation of Yugoslavia gives no idea of the losses, sufferings, the effort, quarrels, triumphs, welter of human emotion, that went into the making of it. Economic losses through destruction of property, of communications, land and agricultural production, were so great as to be difficult to estimate, and there was no United Nations economic aid to destroyed and under developed countries after the First World War.

The emotion generated by the Yugoslav movement and the speed with which its objectives were achieved towards the end of the war resulted in almost every decision – agreements between Serbs, Croats, Slovenes, as well as between Yugoslavs and their neighbours – being taken in a spirit of heated partisanship. Above all the South Slav movement had not had mass support from the general body of people, the peasants, who were preoccupied with economic problems. The past history of every group of South Slavs had given no training in the art of judicial compromise, in the discipline required when people with different views must work together to achieve unity. Inevitably a long time would be needed to create a Yugoslav nation. Both internal and external circumstances in the period following the First World War made this task exceptionally difficult.

The outstanding problem of the new state was to find a form of government acceptable to all groups of South Slavs. This was never achieved during the inter-war period. The Serbs wanted a centralized state with its capital at Belgrade (in Serbia), its dynasty and institutions to be the same as those of pre-1914 Serbia. Croats and other nationalities wanted autonomy in a federal state. These ideas were incompatible. They were argued by leaders on both sides with an intransigeance that excluded compromise. No significant concessions were made before 1941 when Germany invaded and occupied Yugoslavia and the state disintegrated.

The new kingdom was comparatively large (98,767 square miles) with a population of about 12,000,000 inhabitants.[23] Serbia had a population of nearly $5\frac{1}{2}$ million; Croatia (including Slavonia and Dalmatia) 3,360,000, Bosnia-Hercegovina 1,890,000, Slovenia 1,055,000 and Montenegro 199,000.[24] Although Serbia had suffered terrible losses during the war, she was still, because of her greater area and larger population, in a stronger position than the other regions when it came to arguments about government. More/over Serbia was the only region to have an army and the skeleton of a civil service left over from her pre/war state. The army at this time, as after the Second World War, was a powerful political weapon.

A parliament was elected in 1920 (by suffrage of males over twenty/one) to work out a constitution. Significantly most of the party groups in this parliament were associated with a region. The two strongest parties, Democrats (94) and Radicals (93), were based on pre/war Serbian parties; the third largest group, Communists (58), were the only party to have support on a non/regional basis in spite of their extreme programme for revolutionary changes on the lines of recent developments in the new state of Soviet Russia.

It rapidly became apparent that no agreement about a constitution could be reached. The Serbs wanted a centralized state that would have fulfilled their dream of 'greater Serbia'. The Croats who were mostly represented by the Croat Peasant Party (50 deputies) pro/posed autonomy for each region with only limited powers for the central government. Stephen Radić, leader of the Croat Peasant Party, was a brilliant demagogue with a large following among peasants in Croatia.[25] His policy and outlook were narrowly in the interests of Croatia, especially those of the peasants. He never became a leader of more than regional outstanding, but he was immensely popular in Croatia. He received some tactical support from Father Korošec, an able Catholic priest, leader of the Slovene Peoples Party. Father Korošec wanted some autonomy for Slovenia where he envisaged political power being in the hands of the Catholic Church; he later compromised with the Serbs in order to gain concessions for this policy.

The most powerful political personality among the Serbs was King Alexander who had the support of the octogenarian Serbian politi/cian Nikola Pašić. The King was by character and training un/fitted to deal with a situation that required tact, diplomacy, and a genuine desire for compromise. Educated at the Czarist officers' school in St Petersburg and in the Serbian army he was both auto/cratic and intensely Serbian. He had neither experience of nor belief in parliamentary government.

On 28 June 1921 (Vidovdan or St Vitus day), the Serbian proposal for government was forced through parliament. 223 deputies (nearly all Serbs) voted for the constitution, 35 voted against and 161 (including Croat Peasant Party, Serbian Peasant Party, Slovene Peoples' Party and Communist deputies) abstained. The Croats had already retired to Zagreb and refused to participate in the assembly. Some months before the passing of the constitution, Communist Party and Trade Union activities had been outlawed (30 December 1920). The Vidovdan constitution was in all major respects the same as that of pre-war Serbia. It gave great powers to the king and his own appointed executive. Parliament was left little power to control or initiate acts of government, though it was free to debate and criticize. It rapidly degenerated into a forum for political intrigue and personal vendetta.

The Vidovdan constitution lasted eight years. The composition of government changed frequently but was always predominantly Serb, for the King used his full constitutional rights to promote a pro-Serb government. As political life became more embittered he came to believe that only Serbs, and a few other politicians who could be bribed or suborned, could be relied on to carry out his policies. Thus Serbs filled almost all high offices in government, army, banking and finance. This increased the bitterness of other nationalities and led to violence and increased repression in public life.

In 1924, Radić, after three years abstention returned to parliament in an attempt to form a united opposition with other opponents of the régime, but this too failed. Everybody in public life felt frustrated and dissatisfied. The opposition were powerless to get a hearing for their views, let alone change official policy. Supporters of the king quarrelled so much among themselves that governments had to be reformed with a frequency that made stable government impossible. These conditions seemed to King Alexander only further proof that parliamentary government was undesirable.

In June 1928 during one of many quarrels in parliament, a Montenegrin deputy shot down Radić (who died shortly after) and two other members of the Croat Peasant Party. The ensuing crisis ended the period of government under the Vidovdan constitution.

The Croat Peasant Party under its new leader Vladko Maček again seceded from parliament. In January 1929, King Alexander suspended the constitution and began a period of dictatorship lasting till his death.

For nearly three years the King ruled without a constitution; political parties were abolished, backed by a drastic Defence of the Realm Act which allowed the death penalty for many 'offences'. The judiciary was even less independent than before; local government was reorganized and new provinces were created to run across the old regions to which people had shown such strong allegiance.

In 1931 the King issued a new constitution providing for election of a parliament (two chambers) with severely restricted powers. All parties were banned except an official government party and all power was still in the hands of the King. Still nothing was done to compromise with the Croats whose demands were becoming more extreme as Serbian hegemony increased. A few Croats began to support a group of fanatical chauvinists called Ustaše who had established connections with the fascists in Italy. Members of this party organized the murder of King Alexander (by a Macedonian terrorist) when he made an official visit to France in 1934.

Alexander's death postponed solution of the basic constitutional problem for another seven years, for his heir, Prince Peter was a fourteen-year-old minor. King Alexander's will nominated three regents of whom his cousin, English educated Prince Paul Karadjordjević was the most important.[26] Prince Paul remained effective ruler in Yugoslavia until 1941. He did nothing to stop the intrigues and corruption of public life and continued the pro-Serb dictatorship of Alexander, stating that changes could not be made until the King came of age. After 1934, internal politics developed against the background of Hitler's threat to Europe. Although this held increasing dangers for Yugoslavia, it did not help to unite the two main protagonists, Serbs and Croats.

Government under the dictatorship was no more stable than it had been before; from 1929 to 1941 Yugoslavia had 7 prime ministers, 15 cabinets in which 121 ministers served (who all received a ministerial pension after one year's service). Of the 121 ministers, 73 were Serbs, 33 Croats, 10 Slovenes and 5 Bosnian Moslems.[27] Public life continued to be notorious for its graft, nepotism and corruption. The electoral law of 1931 allowed for opposition votes to be registered, but operated so that the government party always had a large majority in parliament. Voting was by open ballot and police intimidation and bribery were commonplace.

The Prime Minister who held power longest was Milan Stojadinović (1935–8). Increasing Nazi and Fascist pressure on Yugoslavia offered further opportunities for personal advancement (and enrichment) to those who were prepared to work for German and Italian interests. Stojadinović was one of them. Prince Paul himself also became increasingly pro-axis.

Even before the Nazis, Yugoslavia's position in foreign affairs had been precarious and difficult. Shortly after the First World War settlement Yugoslavia had allied herself with other new states of central Europe to protect herself against possible claims for revision of frontiers by Hungary, Bulgaria, Austria and Italy. The alliance (Little Entente) with Czechoslovakia (1920) and Rumania (1921) led to successful economic and cultural co-operation, but was never an effective international force. Yugoslavia refused all diplomatic relations with communist Russia.

In 1934 Yugoslavia tried to strengthen her security system by joining Greece, Turkey and Rumania in a Balkan Pact and even made overtures to Bulgaria to try to end mutual hostility, but this had little result. In the same year, Yugoslavia with the Little Entente joined in the League of Nations economic sanctions against Italy for invading Abyssinia. Italy was one of Yugoslavia's main trading partners, and sanctions which failed in their objective of weakening Italy, lost Yugoslavia a large part of her export and import trade. This marked the end of Yugoslavia's reliance on small power solidarity. From this time until the outbreak of war, Yugoslavia was drawn more and more into the German economic and political system.

Economic conditions had an important influence on political life. In general, the whole country was underdeveloped, some regions were more backward, and life in some parts was extremely primitive. Inevitably a great part of the revenue for underdeveloped regions had to come from the more developed provinces of Croatia and Slovenia. This was an added cause of grievance.

An outstanding problem in the newly liberated regions of Croatia-Slavonia, Vojvodina and Dalmatia, Bosnia-Hercegovina and Macedonia, was the need for land reform. Feudal conditions were different in each region, and the problem was exacerbated by quarrels about an equitable solution and by the tremendous administrative difficulties of reform. This was eventually carried out piecemeal, partly during the nineteen-twenties, part during the dictatorship; there were separate regulations for the different regions.

Over the whole period, more than 5 million acres (2 million hectares) of land (exclusive of woodland) were distributed amongst 637,000 households. The average holding was very small, and though the reform solved a crying social injustice it did not solve the problem of peasant poverty.[28]

Peasant ownership led to some increased production and yields rose slowly during the inter-war period. But the rate of increase did not keep pace with the rapid growth of population. In many areas malnutrition among peasants was endemic, downright starvation a frequent occurrence. Between 1919 and 1930 about 250,000 (including those who returned, and they numbered over 95,000) emigrated. From 1931 to 1939 the figure was about 105,000, of whom over 80,000 returned. Emigrants' remittances formed an important item in Yugoslavia's foreign currency receipts.[29]

There were many reasons for continued rural poverty. Holdings were small; peasants ignorant (the great majority illiterate), conservative, in debt and too poor to afford investment for improved farming. Some government support in loans and credit was given to peasant co-operative societies. But this was on too small a scale and suffered from political intrigue and corruption. Long term policy and comprehensive improvements that demanded heavy investment and an educated co-operative peasantry were not forthcoming. Relations between peasants and government deteriorated, especially after 1931 during the years of the depression. Many peasants on becoming owners had increased their grain production. During the nineteen-thirties grain fetched starvation prices and became difficult to sell at a time when prices of industrial goods were increasing. Selling cheap and buying dear-peasants could not hope to win through to prosperity. This was one of the reasons why, during the Second World War, many peasants supported Tito's Partisans whose movement they thought would lead to social and economic revolution.

In industry too, in the inter-war years, the picture was one of an underdeveloped nation – underdeveloped in spite of rich natural resources. Confidence in Yugoslavia's political stability was not strong enough to attract foreign capital on the scale that would have been necessary and in any case the government was too preoccupied with political and personal issues and too ignorant to undertake economic planning. Industrial exploitation was left to private developers and was mostly in foreign hands. French interests in the Bor copper mines and British in the Trepča lead mines of pre-war Serbia continued. Ores were mainly exported in unrefined state. Some development was made, mainly for armaments, in the existing steel industry.

The picture of Yugoslavia's export trade in these years reflects the agricultural and industrial position. Trade with Yugoslavia's Little Entente and Balkan Allies was small because their economies were similar. Trade with France and Great Britain was small because of distance and Yugoslavia's difficulty in providing products of suitable quality. Natural trading partners, both for ease of communications and complementary economies, were Italy, Austria and Germany. This made Yugoslavia an easy prey when economic penetration became a political weapon of Nazi Germany.

In 1934 a new important trade agreement with the Nazis led to Germany obtaining a stranglehold on Yugoslav economic life and a powerful influence on her politics. Germany offered Yugoslavia prices above those of the world market for grain and other agricultural products, and was willing to buy as much as the Yugoslavs could produce. Under a clearing agreement, payment was to be made in goods from Germany. But the goods Yugoslavia most needed were not made available and the blocked marks were liquidated by imports of unsuitable and unnecessary goods.

Germany had already acquired considerable financial interests in

Yugoslav industry and banking. After the Anschluss she added the interests of Austrian and German companies, which gave her decisive control even over Yugoslavia's armaments industries and imports. Simultaneously, by exhortation and blackmail Germany was activating the half million strong German minority in Yugoslavia in order to use it as a Trojan horse when occupation of the Balkans became necessary. By the outbreak of war in 1939 Yugoslavia was a helpless economic and almost a political satellite of the Nazis.

Between 1939 and 1941 Yugoslavia was formally neutral though increasing pressure was put on her leaders to join the axis. Stojadinović was relieved of his position as premier after the 1938 election and interned in February 1939, less for his pro-Italian and pro-Nazi activities than because he was thought to be organizing a coup that would make him Yugoslav Führer. Dr Dragiša Cvetković, who became premier in 1938, and Prince Paul had both decided that Germany was too strong to be opposed. Though German occupa-tion of Yugoslavia seemed inevitable, they hoped (however un-realistically) to limit dismemberment for which Italy, Hungary and Bulgaria had long been pressing, and retain a Yugoslav state. On 7 April 1939, Mussolini's forces occupied Albania; a war in which Yugoslavia would be involved was now virtually a certainty yet Croats and Serbs were still in disagreement. Maček under heavy pressure from some Croat elements and from Italy to secede from Yugoslavia and declare a separate state of Croatia had been nego-tiating for months with the Serbs who still refused his demands for self-government.[30] It was not until 23 August 1939 that an agree-ment, the Sporazum, was signed. By this time it was too late to help bring about a united Yugoslav state. A new government was formed with Maček as vice-premier. The Sporazum had allowed Croatia-Dalmatia to become an autonomous administrative unit under its own *Ban*, or governor. It was to have its legislature in Zagreb and its own budget. The central government retained control of national defence, foreign affairs, internal security, foreign trade, transport, religion, education policy, mining, insurance and weights and measures. Autonomous powers were thus not dangerously wide had the agreement taken place in peace-time conditions, or at the beginning of the kingdom. As it was, the Second World War broke out only a few days later, on 1 September 1939. There were still many Serbs who believed that concessions to Croats had gone too far, and many Croats whose mistrust of Serbs and experience of Serb hegemony had been so bitter that they preferred a completely independent Croatia.

In October 1940 the axis ring round Yugoslavia was completed when Italy invaded Greece. Successful Greek resistance made it necessary for Germany to send military aid to the Italians, and for Yugoslavia this posed the vital question. Should she give aid to her ally in the Balkan pact or accede to German demands for passage of troops through Yugoslavia? Government policy was never in doubt. Whilst popular demonstrations were taking place in Belgrade and other Yugoslav towns against support for the axis, Premier Cvetković and Foreign Minister Cincar-Marković journeyed to Vienna to sign the Tripartite Pact whose secret clauses gave Germany the right of passage of troops through Yugoslavia. On 27 March 1941 a *coup d'état* overthrew the regency, declared Peter II to be of age (he was to be eighteen in the following September) and replaced the government of Cvetković by one under General Dušan Simović. The new government did not proclaim a very different policy from that which it replaced. But it was not allowed time to establish itself.

The revolution received popular support especially in Serbia in spite of the certainty of German vengeance. It was to salute this supreme act of courage that Winston Churchill told the British parliament that Yugoslavs had 'saved the soul and the future of their country'.[31] On 6 April Germany invaded Yugoslavia and on 17 April with the country virtually occupied and government, King and leaders already in exile, the Yugoslav army capitulated.

In the war years that followed, the Communist Party emerged to play a vital part, yet in 1918 when the Kingdom of Yugoslavia was established it did not exist at all.

Up to 1918, left wing political supporters in Serbia and South Slav regions of Austro-Hungary had belonged to Social Democratic parties. They had no united programme, and individuals varied widely in their attitude to Marxism (favoured by the Serbian political thinker Svetozar Marković) and to the different groups of German socialism. Before the First World War, Trade unions began to appear in the industrial areas of Croatia, Slovenia and Bosnia-Hercegovina. After the war, economic depression and the Russian revolution as well as the brief communist success in Hungary encouraged their further development.

In 1919 a congress was held in Belgrade (20–23 April) which was attended by representatives of the Serbian Democratic Party, and some members of the Social Democratic parties of Bosnia-Hercegovina, Croatia-Slavonia and Dalmatia, and the Vojvodina. A joint party, the Socialist Workers' Party (Communist) of Yugoslavia was set up. Resolutions were passed accepting the Marxist interpretation of socialism and calling for extension of the party's activities among the working people and peasants of Yugoslavia.

A second congress was held at Vukovar in the following year (20–25 July 1920) where the party's name was changed to the Communist Party of Yugoslavia. At this congress it was evident that strong disagreement existed among members about whether party work should be active, using strikes, demonstrations, even violence, or whether more Fabian tactics should be adopted. The party secretary Sima Marković was in favour of the latter policy because the employers, backed by a powerful state police, were too strong for the workers. Failure of strikes in Zagreb and Slovenia seemed to prove his point. But many militant communists were against him and support amongst the workers was increasing in that time of post-war unemployment and low wages.[32] The Communist Party put forward candidates in many local elections and won control of the town councils of Zagreb, Belgrade and five other towns in Serbia. Fearful that Yugoslavia might follow the pattern of Hungary where communists had gained control, Drašković, Minister of the Interior of the Yugoslav Provisional Government, took strong measures against strikers and communists. In spite of this the communists came out third strongest party at the general election in October 1920. Alarmed by the strength of communist support the government issued a proclamation on 30 December 1920 (the Obzana) which outlawed Communist Party and trade union activities. Their publications were forbidden and property confiscated; the party went underground and remained illegal to the outbreak of the Second World War. Many of its leaders were arrested, others went into exile.[33] In 1921 it had claimed a membership of 60,000; by 1929 it was reduced to 3,500 and still dwindling.[34]

The party continued to exist but was split into warring factions which could not agree on policy; it was directed by the Communist International (Comintern) in Moscow, which it had joined immediately after its inception in 1919, through leaders who lived outside Yugoslavia and were often ill-informed about, and at logger-heads with the underground party. The party was easily infiltrated by police spies; communists who remained active were often arrested and imprisoned.

The major subject of disagreement continued to be the question of active or passive resistance. Communist newspapers (*Borba, Radnik, Delo* and others) still appeared sporadically, and a new legal political party was formed, the Independent Workers' Party (NRPJ). This received little support in the election of March 1923 (1·1 of votes), and ceased to exist after being banned in 1924.

Two other subjects of disagreement were what line to take about the position of nationalities within the state of Yugoslavia – should the communist line support centralism or demand autonomy for Croats, Slovenes, Macedonians and other groups in the state? – and the further question of what should be the communist attitude to-wards the peasants – should they be wooed by communists, or ignored and denounced as owners of private land which communists hoped to nationalize? There was also the problem of how relations should be regulated between party and Trade Unions. Some of these questions were resolved by resolutions taken at underground con-ferences, but many communists remained unconvinced by majority decisions which party discipline was too weak to enforce, and a generally accepted programme for the party was not effectively worked out until communists came to power during the war.

Party conferences continued to be held during the nineteen twenties (in Vienna in 1922 and 1923, twice in Belgrade in 1923) and two congresses (more important than the conferences) were held, one in 1926 in Vienna (the Third Party Congress) and the other in 1928 in Dresden (the Fourth Party Congress). This was the last congress to be held until 1948. During these years party secretaries were changed as one faction after another gained power; Marković, gaoled in 1921 and released in 1923, was restored on the orders of the Comintern in 1926, he had little support among the active Party workers inside Yugoslavia and was replaced in 1928 by the Bosnian Djuro Djaković whose death at the hands of the police in the following year was followed by further disagreement on who should be secretary.

These quarrels in the Yugoslav Communist Party, the lack of discipline, excessive independence of local parties in the main areas of the country, were problems that continued to exercise the Comintern in Moscow. They were extremely difficult to resolve as Yugoslav communists then, as later under Tito, were resentful of foreign interference even though it came from Moscow; at the same time they were too inexperienced to solve their own difficulties, for they had been forced underground before the party had had time to organize itself, and conditions for illegal activity in Yugoslavia were extremely harsh. The Comintern sent a stream of advice, threats, warnings and emissaries to Yugoslavia to little effect. The Third Party Congress in Vienna (June 1926) reached apparent agreement on all issues, with decisions in favour of supporting autonomy for the nationalities and trying to gain support from the peasants. Yet by 1928, the party was again so splintered into factions that the Comintern sent another delegation to investigate it. This inquiry was prompted by a letter drafted at a meeting of thirty-two delegates of the Zagreb City Communist Group in February 1928 and dispatched with delegates to the Comintern in Moscow; it asked for intervention to put an end to indiscipline and weakness in the Yugoslav Communist Party. One of the conference delegates most active in promoting this letter, was a Croatian Trade Unionist and party member, Josip Brož, later to be called Tito. He had been an active party member for some years past, but now for the first time began to come to the fore.

The Comintern's reaction was a stern Open Letter to the Yugoslav Communist Party. This was presented at the Fourth Party Congress in Dresden in October 1928, after which apparent unanimity was enforced and an entire new leadership, nominated by the Comintern, was elected. But it was not long before the Comintern's nominee as secretary, Djuro Djaković, was picked up by the police, and after his murder, and the inauguration of King Alexander's dictatorship in 1929, the party was for three years virtually in abeyance. By 1932 the party could only count on a membership of 200. During these years a number of communists who were later to become leading figures in the present-day Yugoslav republic, were in gaol; amongst them were Tito himself, Edward Kardelj, Alexander Ranković and Moša Pijade. These four, who were not imprisoned together, ex-perienced some harsh treatment, but were still able to organize communist groups and study Marxism in prison.

In 1932 the Comintern again attempted to resurrect the Yugoslav Communist Party; a new committee was appointed with a new General Secretary, Milan Gorkić. From Vienna they attempted to get local party organizations going again. By 1934 membership had reached 1,000 and was increasing, helped by communists who were released from gaol (among them Tito in 1934). The party benefited from a slight relaxation of political pressure and their work was made easier because the general lack of political liberty in the country brought people to their ranks who might in conditions of greater political freedom have been content to support a less extreme political party.

A regional conference of the party was held in secret in Slovenia in December 1934; eleven delegates were present including Kardelj and Tito, who had organized the conference and helped to draw up the very critical report that was submitted to the delegates. He also helped to draw up instructions for future work for communists to try to win support among young people, students, the peasants, trade unions and in the army and air force. Gorkić was again elected secretary and for the first time Tito was elected to the committee.

For the next two years Tito was in Moscow where he had been ordered to work in the Balkan Secretariat of the Comintern. Here he received reports from Yugoslavia where the party was still divided between supporters of active and passive resistance, with Gorkić (working from his headquarters in Vienna) in favour of the latter policy. By 1936, with the party still disrupted by quarrels, the Comintern decided on another clean-sweep of Yugoslav Communist Party officials. Although Tito disapproved of him, Gorkić had Comintern support and continued as secretary whilst Tito was appointed Organizing Secretary. In his memoirs Tito says that when he travelled to Yugoslavia at this time he refused to use false passports furnished by Gorkić, for he had noted that others who had used them often fell into the hands of the police, and he suspected Gorkić of using this method of eliminating his opponents in the party.[35]

Tito did not immediately take up his organizing work, as he was instructed by the Comintern to mobilize volunteers for the Republican Army in the civil war in Spain. The headquarters of the Yugoslav Communist Party Central Committee was moved to Paris and Tito travelled about Europe organizing underground routes for sending volunteers to Spain. He visited Yugoslavia on a number of occasions for party work and seems to have made a success of both jobs and won the confidence and respect of Stalin and the new leaders in Russia. Tito was fortunate in coming to the fore at this time and not earlier, and in being engaged in work outside Russia. He was not sufficiently important to be involved in Stalin's great purge of 1937.

This purge affected the Yugoslav Communist Party as it did all other communist parties in Europe. It provided the opportunity to eliminate Gorkić and other opponents of active policy for communists in Yugoslavia. Tito was summoned to Moscow, informed that he had been designated Secretary General of the Yugoslav Communist Party and told that the party would be liquidated unless order was restored and maintained. Tito was given a fairly free hand in reorganizing and reforming the party. It is significant and characteristic that nearly all the men chosen by Tito at this time remained with him throughout the war and are still his closest supporters today. The only outstanding exception is Milovan Djilas who was active in communist students' organization in these years.

From the moment he was appointed to a position of power Tito showed outstanding ability and qualities of leadership; party quarrels at last ended and discipline was enforced. It is also characteristic that from the beginning he insisted on the primary importance of building up the Yugoslav Communist Party on a strong national basis with Yugoslav leaders (not foreigners living abroad) and a policy orientated to Yugoslav needs with the ultimate object of obtaining power, however remote that may have appeared then.

In 1937 the party had 1,500 members; in 1939 it had about 6,000 and by the autumn of 1940 claimed 12,000 members with a further 30,000 members of communist youth groups. Party groups began to be organized in all parts of the country. In these years the party reacted strongly to the pro-German policy of Prince Paul and Stojadinović; hatred of Nazism and Fascism joined with nationalism in this attitude and did much to gain increased support for the party. Demonstrations were organized against the Anschluss and each act of Nazi aggression; though the communists appear to have been as much surprised as most other Yugoslavs by the *coup d'état* of 27 March 1941 they demonstrated with many thousands of other Yugoslavs in its favour and against the Tripartite Pact.

Throughout these years the Yugoslav Communist Party continued to look to Soviet Russia for inspiration and support. It is clear that they hoped that one day the Soviet Union would help communism to power in Yugoslavia. The Nazi-Soviet pact must have been very difficult to swallow and the measure of embarrassment it caused is seen in the fact that no Yugoslav communist documents have been published on this matter. Tito went to Moscow late in 1939 and returned to Yugoslavia early in 1940. It is not known what instructions or advice he received, but after this the party line became clear – all out denunciation of the Yugoslav government and neutrality towards the war in Europe which was to be regarded as a war between capitalists. This was officially confirmed at the Fifth Party Conference held in Zagreb from 19 to 23 October 1940.[36]

The German invasion of Yugoslavia gave the opportunity for a rallying call to communists, but there was still no declaration of policy. It seems that decision had been taken to wait on events and prepare the party to fight at some later date, and in circumstances as yet unknown. The party was instructed to prepare for revolt which was to be timed for when it would assist the Soviet Union and thus be most favourable to Yugoslav communism. Tito's struggle for power had entered a new phase.[37]

Meanwhile Yugoslavia virtually disintegrated as a result of invasion, and the Germans lost no time in partitioning the country. Slovenia was divided between Germany (who annexed the northern half adjacent to Austria) and Italy who received Ljubljana and the rest of the province. Italy also received part of Dalmatia including the islands, the city of Split, the naval base of Kotor, and parts of the Dalmatian hinterland. She had military control of Montenegro which was nominally to be independent. Albania, also assigned to Italy, was enlarged to include areas of Yugoslavia inhabited by Albanian minorities in western Macedonia and Kosovo in Serbia. The rest of Macedonia and parts of south Serbia went to Bulgaria, Germany's ally. Hungary received the rich Danubian province of Bačka and two smaller adjoining Yugoslav provinces, Medjumurje and Prekomurje.

The remaining part of Croatia together with Bosnia-Hercegovina was made into a so-called Independent State of Croatia, in theory a kingdom to be ruled by an Italian Prince, the Duke of Spoleto. This prince never took over his kingdom and the state was ruled by Ante Pavelić, leader of the Croatian Fascist movement, the Ustaše. Pavelić enforced his rule with Ustaše troops and German and Italian arms. He introduced a reign of terror with atrocities as vile as anything that happened anywhere in the Second World War. Jews, Serbs and anyone who refused to accept the new state were liquidated in great numbers and by horrifying methods. Orthodox Christians were converted to Catholicism or murdered. Many Croats who had wanted independence were shocked to receive it in this form. Some of the Croat Peasant Party threw in their lot with the Ustaše, some fled abroad. Maček and other leaders stayed on and tried to remain neutral.[38] The Catholic Church in Croatia was in a difficult position, and many priests like Archbishop Stepinac of Zagreb adopted an ambivalent attitude, sometimes identifying themselves with the new state and blessing its troops as they went about their grizzly terrorism, at other times denouncing the slaughter and enforced conversions.

In Serbia, the northern part, inhabited by Volksdeutsche, stayed under local German administration, the rest, under German military control was nominally ruled by a Serbian quisling General Milan Nedić, supported by his own Serbian State Guard and certain Serbian fascist troops led by Dimitrije Ljotić.

Whilst the Germans were organizing dismemberment of the state, the Yugoslav Communist Party with twenty years' experience of underground organization had organized a military committee with its headquarters in Belgrade and dispersed most of its members to different regions of the country to make 'final preparations for the uprising' – when the time was considered ripe.[39] The communists were in radio communication with Moscow by means of a transmitter in Zagreb (a second transmitter in Belgrade had been destroyed in the German bombardment of 6 April).[40]

Hitler's invasion of Russia on 22 June gave the signal for the Yugoslav communists to go over to active resistance. Preparations were well in hand as Tito had known about the coming invasion of Russia since the middle of May.[41] The first acts of sabotage against occupation troops took place in most regions (except Macedonia where difficulties between Yugoslav and Bulgarian communists were not resolved until later) and were directed by Tito from his Belgrade headquarters. By mid-August resistance had become a general revolt in Serbia; Tito's supporters were organized as an army, calling themselves 'Partisans'; regular military bulletins began to be issued. By the end of August the Partisans held much of the countryside outside the main towns in west Serbia, and Tito decided to leave Belgrade.

An important problem faced the communists at this time about their relationship with another very different resistance movement. A Serbian army officer, Draža Mihailović had refused to accept the Yugoslav capitulation and had established himself in the district of Ravna Gora in west Serbia with a number of followers who called themselves *Četniks* (Četnici in Serbian). The political outlook of Mihailović differed greatly from that of the communists. He was a patriotic Serb, devoted to the monarchy, opposed to Croats and communists and eager to see the restoration of the pre-war order in

Yugoslavia. Though personally courageous, he was a weak, almost incapable leader with little control over his followers. In September 1941 proposals were made for joint operations between Četniks and Partisans. Mihailović had already managed to contact the British, and a British liaison officer, Col. Hudson, reached Mihailović in October.[42]

On 27 October Tito's proposals for joint operations, supplies and headquarters were turned down by Mihailović (influenced perhaps by the possibility of allied support), who had no wish to be associated with communists whom he regarded as an enemy as dangerous as the Germans and Italians. Relations between the two groups deteriorated rapidly and it was not long before Partisans and Četniks were fighting each other and Četniks were aiding Germans and Italians in most of the major operations against the Partisans.[43]

Partisan successes in Serbia roused the Germans to retaliate by punitive massacres (7,000 civilian population killed in Kragujevac and 1,700 workers in Kraljevo for example). An offensive of regular troops forced the Partisans out of Serbia into the Sanjak of Novi Pazar and east Bosnia. The Četniks were left undisturbed in Ravna Gora.

The development of the Partisan movement after 1941 was to show the extent of Tito's genius for leadership. He showed both political and military skill and a clear-sighted, determined grasp of the strategy needed for his long-term aim, to gain political power for the Communist Party in a liberated and reunited Yugoslavia. Thus Tito's Partisans became the leaders of a national liberation movement, and his army called itself the Peoples' Army of Liberation. As such it gained support from people of all regions, religions and political views.[44] In 1942 the Partisans increased their numbers (to about 100,000 men and women) in spite of military setbacks. Two German offensives (aided by Italian, Četniks and Ustaše) pushed the Partisans out of Serbia, and defeated them in Montenegro, Hercegovina and east Bosnia. There were few pitched battles. Partisan successes were calculated by how much territory they could control – liberated territory as it was called. By the end of 1942 they still held considerable stretches in the mountains of Bosnia, Croatia and

Dalmatia. In September 1942, though no possibility of ultimate success was in sight, the Partisans began to organize units of military government for all the territory they controlled. A central government was set up and a form of wartime parliament was summoned to meet at Bihać in Bosnia (26 and 27 November 1942). This was called the Anti-Fascist Council of Peoples' Liberation of Yugoslavia (AVNOJ). Seventy-one elected members were summoned from all parts of the country of whom fifty-four were able to attend, many crossing secretly through enemy territory. The term 'elected' was widely interpreted for no real elections could be held, and only communists or their supporters were chosen, usually by local Partisan groups. This Council elected as President Dr Ivan Ribar, a respectable middle-class lawyer, former President of the Yugoslav Constituent Assembly of 1920.[45] An Executive Council was chosen to deal with non-military affairs, with officials to be in charge of education, public health, social welfare, religion, publicity and other matters of civilian administration.

The creation of this government was a challenge to the Yugoslav government in exile which had appointed Mihailović its Minister of War. In January 1943 the Partisans' Executive Council addressed a note to the Allied leaders claiming that it was more representative of the Yugoslav people than the Yugoslav royalist government in exile. On 8 February 1943 it issued a statement of its political aims expressed in very general terms – the liberation and reunion of the country, guarantees of private property and that no radical changes would be made until the end of the war.

The Partisans' Executive Council was faced with tremendous tasks; it had to organize food supplies, some form of traffic control on roads and railways, get industries working, postal services, education, medical and hospital services and collect taxes from the local population. Everything was in short supply. The Partisans showed a genius for improvization and endurance. They were inspired by the reckless courage which South Slavs had shown throughout their history, and by desperate nationalism to which the communists added a fanatical belief in their political cause. Tito was not well known to the masses who joined the Partisan movement. His pre-war underground career had necessitated anonymity. He had been away in Russia for long periods and some people at this time believed him to be a Russian.[46] He had a small group of devoted assistants, most of whom had worked with him for some years and are still working with him today.[47]

The Partisans' claim to be a representative government was a threat which the Germans could not ignore and they made great efforts in 1943 to achieve a military victory which would destroy the whole movement. Two great offensives were mounted, the fourth (January 1943), in which the Partisan forces were pushed out of Croatia across the river Neretva into Bosnia and Montenegro, and the fifth (May to July 1943), which was an attempt to encircle the Partisans who had regrouped in Montenegro in the triangle formed by the Tara and Pliva rivers and mount Durmitor. Both offensives failed. In the fifth offensive, the Partisans succeeded in breaking through the German ring and crossed the Sutjeska river into Bosnia, but they suffered terrible losses,[48] and Tito himself was wounded.

By the summer of 1943 the tide of war was beginning to change – in Yugoslavia as in other theatres of war. A British military mission commanded by Brig. Fitzroy Maclean reached Tito's headquarters in September and organized allied military and medical aid for the Partisan army.[49] In the same month came the Italian capitulation. Tito, angry that the allies had not given him advance information, had to race with the Germans to try to receive the surrender and arms of the Italian forces. The Partisans managed to seize most of the islands and coastland of Dalmatia, much of Italian-held Slovenia (except Ljubljana), Istria (then the Italian province of Venezia Guilia) and most of Montenegro. They also got hold of great quantities of Italian arms and were soon joined by huge numbers of recruits; by the end of the year the Partisan army was numbered at 300,000.

On 29 November 1943 a second meeting of A V N O J was held at Jajce attended by 142 out of 250 representatives from all parts of Yugoslavia. This was a confident and hopeful meeting. Tito was for the first time named as Josip Broz, nominated as President of the newly appointed National Committee of Liberation, and Commander in Chief of the Partisan army. This meeting passed a resolution that it was the true representative government of Yugoslavia, that it, and not the *émigré* government in London, should be negotiated with in all international agreements affecting Yugoslavia.

The Council passed a further resolution that Yugoslavia would be reconstituted on a federal basis, and must include territories formerly held by Italy; it forbade the royalist government to return to Yugoslavia and stated that the question of king and monarchy would be settled by the people of its own will, after the liberation of the whole country. International recognition soon followed. At the Teheran Conference (December 1943) it was agreed that further allied assistance should be given to Tito.

Up to this time, the Partisans had been very disappointed with the attitude of the Soviet Union which had given plenty of advice (through a secret radio link) but had refused even the most urgent and desperate appeals for aid,[50] though later they sent a military mission to Tito's headquarters. Tito had also been bitterly resentful that Moscow had continued to recognize the royalist *émigré* government. Soviet behaviour was to continue to rankle but it enabled Yugoslav communists later to claim, with truth, that they had won their liberation struggle without direct Soviet assistance.

In 1944 the Germans made another desperate attempt to liquidate Tito by a parachute attack on his headquarters at Drvar in Bosnia. Tito escaped (on his birthday, 25 May) and after a forced march was flown out of Bosnia and re-established his headquarters on the Dalmation island of Vis.[51] Tito realized that it was now time to make political plans for the final phases of the war. Negotiations were begun with the royalist government which had realized that a compromise would have to be made with the successful, and powerful Partisan movement. On 16 June 1944 an agreement was signed between Tito and a royalist representative, Dr I. Šubašić. The Tito-Šubašić agreement stipulated that the king would not return to Yugoslavia until a plebiscite had been held to allow the Yugoslav people to choose their own form of government. Tito was recognized as the sole military commander. By the end of the year the king had reluctantly agreed that his royal powers should be exercised by a three-man regency to include Tito and Šubašić.

Tito at this time was struggling to prevent his movement being engulfed not only by the royalist government and their allied supporters, but, equally dangerous for him, by the Red Army and their political commissars. In the summer of 1944 Tito met Winston Churchill in Naples and shortly after flew secretly to Moscow to make arrangements so that the Partisan army could be recognized as an independent force when the Russian troops entered Yugoslavia on their thrust into German-occupied Europe. On 20 October 1944 the Partisan army entered Belgrade with units of the Red Army.

German forces and their quisling supports (Četniks and Ustaše, Nedić and Ljotić men) were now in flight throughout Yugoslavia and the Partisans (about 800,000 strong) were engaged in mopping-up operations, in taking over government and paying off old scores. A most important problem for Tito was still to be settled – the question of the Slav territories that Italy had acquired after the First World War. Tito was determined that these should be recovered for Yugoslavia and sent Partisan detachments to occupy Istria, Trieste and its hinterland. Partisans were fighting in Trieste itself when the second New Zealand division of the Allied Army arrived on 3 May 1945. For some days both armies claimed the town, but eventually under strong allied pressure, Tito's troops were forced to withdraw. An agreement was reached dividing the disputed territory into the western part (Zone A) under allied administration, and the rest (Zone B) in Yugoslav hands, until the allies should decide between the claims of Yugoslavia and Italy.

These events brought a coolness in relations between Tito and the western allies which was increased as Soviet successes persuaded the Yugoslav communist leader that he must revert to his original idea that Soviet help would be the only international support he could expect for the communist state he was now likely to be able to set up in a reunited Yugoslavia.

29 The Austrian Archduke Franz Ferdinand was murdered at Sarajevo by a Bosnian patriot, Gavrilo Princip on 28 June 1914.

30 The near-by bridge over the river Miljačka was called Princip's Bridge to commemorate the event which led to the Austrian invasion of Serbia and precipitated the First World War.

31 The Serbian army was forced to retreat under Austrian attack. In October 1915 they moved with civilians along the Morava River Road.

32 British officers inspect the Serbian troops at Salonica in 1917 by which time the army had been re-grouped and had joined the Allied forces.

33 A young soldier Josip Brož later to become Marshal Tito and President of Yugoslavia fights in the trenches.

34 On 1 December 1918 the Kingdom of Serbs, Croats and Slovenes was formed and Alexander, former Regent of Serbia, became king.

35 (Left to right) Ljuba Davidović (Democrats), Vladko Maček (Croat Peasant Party), and Javon Jovanović (Agricultural Party) were the leaders of the three main opposition parties in the Parliament elected in 1920.

36 In 1929 King Alexander suspended the Constitution and became a dictator. He was murdered in 1934 by a Macedonian terrorist and a member of the Ustaše which had connections with Italian fascists.

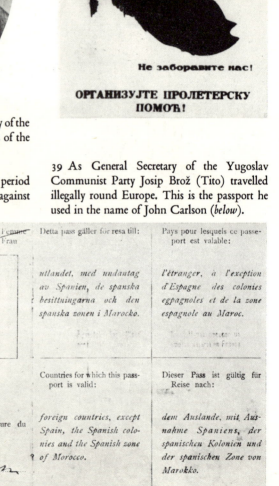

У ПОМОЋ ЖРТВАМА
РЕАКЦИЈЕ!

Не заборавите нас!

ОРГАНИЗУЈТЕ ПРОЛЕТЕРСКУ
ПОМОЋ!

37 Djuro Djaković was General Secretary of the Communist Party and died at the hands of the police in 1929 (*above*).

38 A communist-inspired leaflet of the period urging people to join in the struggle against dictatorship (*above right*).

39 As General Secretary of the Yugoslav Communist Party Josip Brož (Tito) travelled illegally round Europe. This is the passport he used in the name of John Carlson (*below*).

40 Prince Paul, Regent of Yugoslavia until 1941 endorsed the continuation of dictatorship inaugurated by King Alexander. He is seen (centre) with Vladko Maček (left) and Premier Cvetković (right) at Zagreb in 1940.

41 Both Prince Paul and Milan Stojadinović (Premier 1935–8) favoured German and Italian interests. Stojadinović (third from right) visits a state farm in Belje with the Italian Foreign Minister Count Ciano (fourth from right).

42 The Tripartite Pact of 1941 gave Germany the right to move her troops through Yugoslavia. Belgrade demonstrators denounced this treaty and the pro-Nazi government of Premier Cvetković.

43 Yugoslav troops throw down their arms as Nazi guards look on in 1941.

44 A Serbian army officer, Draža Mihailović, formed his own resistance movement. The Četniks, as they were called, opposed the Partisans and eventually collaborated with the Nazis.

45 Ante Pavelić leader of the Croatian Fascist movement inspects his units in 1941. The atrocities which took place at this time were some of the worst during the war.

46 After Germany in-
vaded, Tito organized the
Partisan army and many
acts of sabotage were committed on occupation
armies.

47 Guards of the Peoples'
Army of Liberation at the
lakes of Plitvice in Croatia
in 1943. By this time Tito
had formed a provisional
government.

48 Tito and his colleagues,
many of whom remained
with him throughout the
war, in 1944. Edward
Kardelj is wearing glasses
and stands near Tito.

49 The Central Committee of the Communist Party of Yugoslavia met at their headquarters in Vis in June 1944 by which time it had been accepted as the representative government and Tito appointed President.

50 Tito had a secret meeting with the Prime Minister of Britain, Mr Winston Churchill, at Naples in August 1944 before visiting Moscow to gain the support of the Red Army.

51 In October of the same year soldiers of the National Army of Liberation supported by the Red Army fought for the Liberation of Belgrade.

4   Revolution and After

THE REVOLUTION which took place in Yugoslavia during the Second World War was more fundamental than that brought about by the First World War. This was not only because it brought communists to power. The First World War created a South Slav state, but after the war damage had been cleared up and the form of state decided on, political, social and economic conditions for the vast majority of the people were much the same as before the war. Peasants were as poor, sometimes poorer than they had been before, their opportunities of economic and social improvement, their power to influence political life little greater. Political power was in the hands of the same small class, often the same people, as before the war; the machinery of government of pre-war Serbia was resurrected and imposed on the new state.

The Second World War, even without the communists, was more of a leveller. Enemy destruction, reprisals, occupation affected town and country people alike; except for the few of any class who were prepared to collaborate actively with the enemy, the rigours, deprivations, dangers of war struck without regard to rich or poor, townsmen or peasant. If anything the peasants had the advantage over townspeople, for their production of food was vital to the German war effort. Of incalculable importance was the fact that experiences of war were basically the same for all nationalities in the country – even though some parts were fought over more savagely than others, some occupied by Germans, some by Italians or Bulgarians; in spite of civil war and a divided country, all Yugoslavs were in it together.

The importance of the part played by Tito and his communists cannot be overestimated. They provided the only fighting lead against an occupying enemy; they appealed to all nationalities, were not associated with the Serbs or Croats or with any of the discredited pre-war policies. They were helped by the fact that Tito, whose origins were never stressed, was a Croat rather than a Serb. The communists were also outside the field of Catholic-Orthodox religious rivalry which ran deep in South Slav life and divided pre-war Yugoslavia. Above all the lead given by the Partisans in the fight for freedom made the strongest possible appeal to many Yugoslavs; it appealed to their love of country, of freedom, to the atavistic desire to defend soil and family; it provided the only unequivocal lead in a heroic fight which was of a piece with the long history of South Slav struggle for freedom.

Most communist leaders were from the lower ranks of pre-war society, not from the privileged classes, and they offered a vision of a new future of social justice – a cause which peasants in Slovenia, Croatia, Serbia, and all the South Slav lands had yearned, revolted, died for without success for hundreds of years past. This explains why Tito and his Partisans, both during and after the war, had genuine national support from people who were not communists. They also had the supreme advantage of military success which had not been dependent on foreign troops. It is difficult for later genera-tions to understand the euphoria which this success produced in the immediate post-war atmosphere. It was of immense assistance to the communists when they came to organize a new state in Yugoslavia in 1945.

It would be incorrect to speak of communists seizing power at the end of the war, for they had gradually taken over authority as areas of the country were liberated in the later stages of the war. They had also created a rudimentary machinery of central and local govern-ment before the war ended. This government was supported and in many aspects carried on by an army of Partisans – men and women – which it claimed numbered 800,000.

Tito's immediate need in 1945 was to get his government legalized and recognized both inside Yugoslavia and by foreign states. He set about this task with typically ruthless efficiency. A Provisional Government was nominated on 8 March 1945 consisting of repre/ sentatives of A V N O J (twenty), of the royalist government in exile (three), and of Yugoslavia's pre/war political parties (five). Marshal Tito was nominated Minister President; Šubašić, representing the royalist government, became Minister of Foreign Affairs. In August a provisional parliament was summoned. Its members were delegates from all parts of the country chosen or nominated as for the wartime parliaments of A V N O J, with the addition of sixty/eight repre/ sentatives of pre/war political parties and thirteen independent mem/ bers. The following weeks were crucial to the issue of who was to wield power in post/war Yugoslavia.

Although royalist representation in the government was small compared with that of the communists, it had strong support from the Western allies, especially Great Britain and the United States, and Tito believed that he was likely to come under increasing Western pressure to allow the return of the monarchy with a Western/type democratic constitution. He realized that this would mean the liquidation of his Communist Party. The Soviet Union was too occupied at this time with its own gigantic post/war problems to take any active part in Yugoslav politics; but Tito must have realized that if royalist government of a pre/war type were restored in Yugoslavia, the Soviet Union would ultimately intervene (in spite of the Yalta agreement that Yugoslavia was to be divided as a sphere of influence between East and West on a fifty/fifty basis), and the Yugoslav Communist Party would lose its independence and become a satellite of Soviet Russia. Tito thus faced the double danger and acted swiftly to consolidate his position.

Arrangements were made for a general election to be held in November and the whole weight of the Communist Party and Partisan movement was thrown into ensuring that the vote should be in favour of Tito's party; the National Liberation Movement as it was called, the Communist Party as it was in reality. The movement was riding high on a wave of popularity; Tito himself was a national hero; in the eyes of many people the royalist government was dis/ credited for it had not shared the sufferings of the people in the country and had continued its bitter Serb-Croat feuds throughout the war. Tito made the most of these advantages.

There were other dangers in the internal situation which an election open to all parties and interests might have let loose on the country – national rivalries between Serb and Croat, Macedonian separatism, religious rivalries between Orthodox and Catholic, bitter hatred and personal feuds between those who had worked for, and those who had suffered from the enemy during the war. The country had disintegrated with alarming speed at the beginning of the war, its divisions had been prised further apart by German policy during the war. It was not likely to knit together easily in 1945. Tito took no chances and had no need of outside help to control the situation. No opportunity or facilities were allowed to any political party, racial or religious group to canvass support in the election. The Communist Party concealed its identity and detailed aims behind a monolithic political organization called the Peoples' Front and massive propaganda was used to persuade people to support it. The three members of the royalist government (Grol, Šubašić and Šutej), frustrated by their enforced impotence, resigned before the election was held.

An electoral law of 10 August 1945 gave the vote to all citizens over eighteen, and all enlisted men and women regardless of age; it disenfranchised collaborators, giving the opportunity for many potential opponents, who were accused but not necessarily proved to have collaborated, to lose their vote. The election was held (for a two-chamber parliament) on 11 November 1945 on a single list of National Front candidates. Votes were recorded by dropping a ball in sealed ballot boxes; a box was provided for opposition votes. Foreign observers were invited to witness that the election was held without duress. The Peoples' Front gained 90·48 per cent of votes cast for the Federal Council, 88·68 per cent of votes for the second chamber, the Council of Nationalities. This gave Tito the recognition and legal mandate that he needed to go ahead with the organization of a new state based on communist principles. Foreign recognition of his government followed.

The new parliament met on 29 November 1945. It abolished the monarchy (still popular in parts of Serbia) and proclaimed the Federal Peoples' Republic of Yugoslavia. The six republics, declared autonomous in certain fields of government, were the traditional divisions of the country – Serbia, Croatia, Slovenia, Bosnia/Hercegovina, Montenegro and Macedonia; Serbia was to include an autonomous province, Vojvodina, and an autonomous region, Kosovo/Metohija. These are still the federal republics which to/gether constitute the Republic of Yugoslavia.

The parliament was not used as a policy/making body. Its function was to pass automatically and increasingly without question (Dragoljub Jovanović was imprisoned in 1946 after repeatedly criticizing government policy) laws proposed by the Executive Committee which was composed of leaders of the Communist Party, though this was not publicized at the time and Communist Party membership and activities were concealed. Many important laws were passed by this parliament.

Some, together with a great number of executive decrees, dealt with the organization of relief – feeding, clothing, housing people in the shattered and chaotic post/war conditions; others attempted to lay the foundations of a new state based on communist principles. Laws passed by the Provisional Government were confirmed – amongst these being currency reform (a new currency replaced all old currencies in a ratio of 1 new to 10 old dinars), and the con/fiscation of property of 'state enemies' (e.g. collaborators and Volksdeutsche/Germans who, though Yugoslav nationals, had gone over to the Nazis during the war). Of outstanding importance were the Land Reform laws limiting land holdings of private individuals to 45 hectares (111·12 acres), of churches and other foundations to 10 hectares (24·7 acres); peasant debts were also liquidated. All large and company industries were nationalized in 1945; privately owned industries, except for those employing no outside labour, were nationalized in the following year.

The principles on which the state was to be based were formulated in a constitution passed on 31 January 1946. This was similar to the 1936 constitution of the Soviet Union.[52] It defined (in article 2) the republics of the country (mentioned above) and specified the form and responsibilities of central, regional (in the six republics) and local government. Central government was to be by executive and bi-cameral legislature elected by the people (one representative to 50,000 votes) with the same pattern of elected government for local assemblies in the republics. The powers of central and local government organs were declared to be subject to the law of the land (article 9). Central government had responsibility for foreign policy, defence, security, communications, economic planning and undertakings, budget appropriations, taxation, trade, civil and criminal law (article 44). Although this left education and health as major matters for republican responsibility, it was clear that the regional republics were not to be allowed any autonomous powers which could be used for separatist or anti-communist activities.

The constitution confirmed the limitation of private land holding (article 19 stated 'the land belongs to those who cultivate it') and the nationalization of industry, banking, insurance and foreign trade, on the principle that the means of production belonged to the people (all foreign-held property was nationalized against small compensation in April 1948). A number of liberal democratic principles were laid down including equality of rights for all citizens, freedom of religion, of speech, association and assembly (articles 21-43) the right to work and education, and protection of the law for all citizens. This constitution remained in being until 1952 when it was superseded by a new Fundamental Law, which in turn was replaced by a new constitution in 1963.

The 1946 constitution contained many items that were not, and some that could not, be put into effect in the conditions existing in Yugoslavia at the time. Economic conditions were desperate; food was scarce, housing totally inadequate, disease rampant with medical supplies lacking, and communications so disrupted that it was difficult to get either supplies or government instructions to many parts of the country. The effort required from the whole population to restore normal conditions in the shortest possible time brought much hardship and put many limitations on individual liberty. The United Nations Relief and Reconstruction Administration provided 425,000,000 dollars' worth of aid in the form of food, medical supplies, livestock, machinery and transport. It provided a small number of expert personnel; the main work of reconstruction was done by the Yugoslavs themselves. Underfed, overworked, inexpert and with inadequate materials they reconstructed houses, bridges, roads, railways and revived their existing industries.

The system of government in the early years of the Republic did not last long. It proved to be in many ways unsatisfactory and was highly unpopular. It was amended and reformed and eventually, after Yugoslavia's quarrel with Russia in 1948, it was superseded after 1952 by a new system, which in its turn has experienced many changes. The idealistic theories behind the early government were that it must be a complete break with the past, it must be an expression of the peoples' will, a form of 'democratic socialism' based on Marxist-Leninist principles. Yugoslav communists had no experience of government except in their war-time administration of liberated areas; they had only one communist state, the USSR, to use as a model, and their early institutions were adapted from those of Russia which was still under Stalinist rule. Yugoslav communists at that time still accepted Soviet practice as the authoritative expression of true Marxist-Leninism.

The basis of state authority was the Peoples' Committee (*savet*) which was elected by voters in each area of a hierarchy of districts of increasing size, into which the country was divided for local government. At the bottom of the pyramid was the *opština*, a village or group of villages and hamlets; above this came the *srez* or district which covered small towns and a number of *opštine*; until 1947 there existed two further divisions, the *okrug* (circuit), and the *oblast* (region) but these were soon abolished as redundant. Cities had their own Peoples' Committees, and were subdivided into *rejoni* each with its own committee. Over these came the six republics (plus the two autonomous provinces of Serbia) which had their own Peoples' Committees and elected parliaments. Above all was the federal government with its parliament (*skuptišna*), and the powerful Executive Committee, or cabinet, composed of heads of the various ministries and ministers without portfolio. In this system each larger division had authority over the smaller ones, except in those few matters where the republic had autonomous powers and had final authority over its various subdivisions.

The work of the Peoples' Committees at all levels was very varied. Although mainly concerned with implementing laws and instructions from the central authority, it gave more responsibility, more opportunity for variation and limited initiative, than was exercised at that time by members of parliament. Peoples' Committees had to deal with all local services, with the collection and assessment of taxes, with the organization of compulsory labour service and compulsory deliveries of agricultural produce, which were both highly unpopular features of the first difficult years. When the government decided to press the peasants to form co-operative farms, the Peoples' Committees were responsible for putting them into effect. They were also the channels for 'political education' – much of it communist propaganda, some elementary instruction in civic responsibility, in public health, hygiene and social education. It was estimated that over 50 per cent of people were illiterate in 1945. Providing classes to teach adults to read and write was only one of many education problems which committees at all levels had to deal with, for schools, technical colleges, universities were all inadequate.

In practice Peoples' Committees were too unwieldy to deal with their multifarious tasks. They met infrequently and their authority was exercised by small Executive Committees with paid full-time chairmen and secretaries and some full-time officials. These were almost invariably communists or communist supporters, and in many parts of the country they used their new authority to discriminate against non-communists and even against those (and they were many) who showed open dislike of the new laws. The country lacked able and experienced administrators; it was short of educated and literate people. Many of those with pre-war education and experience were suspected by the communists whose fanaticism in these years regarded any non-communist connected with pre-war bourgeois society as a potential enemy. Although numbers of the latter were small, some were hostile to the régime and only too willing to sabotage the system. Thus the few communists ran local as well as central government; they became the new *élite*, exercising great power with varying degrees of ruthlessness and efficiency.

In spite of all, much was achieved in these years, but at great cost in human suffering. Food was scarce, for harvests were poor and peasants' reaction to government policy of forced purchase, land reform and collectivization was to keep whatever food they could hide for themselves. Consumer goods were very scarce; the few made in the country were of poor quality and foreign trade was too little to provide for their purchase abroad. Such foreign currency as was available was rightly assigned to such priorities as raw materials, medical and educational supplies, food and transport equipment. There was much discontent. Yugoslavs were forbidden to go abroad because of the shortage of manpower, particularly amongst the small numbers of pre-war middle class and richer peasants. A few managed to escape. The majority of Yugoslavs worked and endured.

One of the worst aspects of these years was the harshness of the political climate. Frequent mention has been made above of communists, but in fact great secrecy was maintained in these early years about communist membership and activities. The party worked through the Peoples' Front, allegedly non-party, but intended as a means of organizing support for the government; people were pressed into membership and attendance at political meetings. Membership by 1948 had risen to about eight million; no figures were given for membership of the Communist Party, but in 1948 it was revealed to be 468,175.[53]

Political harshness extended to the law courts (Peoples' Courts which were also short of trained officials) where anyone who owned property (housing had not been nationalized) or could be considered as a member of the pre-war bourgeoisie could not be certain of obtaining justice. Many such people were sent to gaol in these early years before 1948 for alleged (sometimes, certainly, proven) subversive activities, or only for speaking against the government. Police spies and informers were everywhere and the secret political police (UDBa) extremely powerful. These were features of the Stalinist conception of a communist state which the Yugoslav communists had felt it their duty to copy.

There were also many other reasons for strong centralization, for the excessive use of police and militia. Yugoslav leaders knew that their revolution was still insecure, threatened by internal and external enemies – or a combination of both, they knew too that their policies were unpopular. Post-war conditions would have been hard under any government; some communist policies, both the purely ideological ones such as nationalization and collectivization, and those which aimed at long-term improvement as in the development of heavy industry, made life more difficult for ordinary people and increased discontent.

This insecurity was aggravated by the deterioration in Yugoslavia's relations with the outside world – especially with Great Britain and the United States. This was partly due to Yugoslav resentment at continued Allied occupation of Zone A and uncertainty about Zone B, the areas claimed by both Italy and Yugoslavia; no settlement was reached about these until 1953. Frontier incidents aggravated a tense situation and there was an ever present danger of war. Tito was determined to fight rather than lose both zones, and in this at least he had the whole Yugoslav people behind him. Thirty per cent of the annual budget was spent on building up the army and other defence services.

In the fanatical climate of Yugoslav communism at this time everything capitalist and Western was condemned; cultural relations were with other communist states. All contacts with the capitalist West were reduced to a minimum. Western hostility to Yugoslav communism was also increasing as Russia extended her grip over eastern Europe and the cold war intensified. In September 1947 Yugoslavia participated in the foundation of an organization of the communist parties of the Soviet Union, Poland, Rumania, Bulgaria, Hungary, Czechoslovakia, France and Italy. This was called the Cominform, and its headquarters were in Belgrade.

By 1947 the government had decided to launch a Five Year Economic Plan for Yugoslavia, again emulating the Soviet Union. This aimed at rapid industrialization, and was to be dependent for success on foreign aid and trade. More than 50 per cent of Yugoslav trade was already with the Soviet Union and other east European communist countries. This was to be extended, and further loans and credits were arranged with Russia. A number of Soviet experts were already in Yugoslavia helping to train much needed technicians. It seemed a natural political assumption that the struggling new communist state of Yugoslavia should get friendly help from the mighty and established communist state of the Soviet Union.

This illusion of friendship between Soviet and Yugoslav communist parties was shattered by the announcement on 28 June 1948 that Yugoslavia had been expelled from the Cominform. This precipitated an open quarrel which led to fundamental changes in Yugoslav communist theory and practice of government, and profoundly affected the history of world communism. The quarrel was carried on through an exchange of violently critical letters between the two communist parties.[54] These revealed that tension and disagreement had been mounting since the end of the war. Letters were wordy, almost incoherent, and charged with emotion, and as in quarrels between individuals, incidents and resentments from past history were resurrected. The main issue in the quarrel was not made explicit in the letters that were published.

After the quarrel had led to open rupture and the heat of the conflict had died down, Tito gave his definition of the basic issue; 'this conflict between Yugoslavia and the USSR arose from the purely aggressive hegemonistic policy of the USSR towards Yugoslavia, from the attempts to enslave our country economically and politically, to liquidate its independence and to make it into a colony. This conflict began during the war, ripened gradually and the germ of it was marked by unequal relations between the two countries.'[55]

The real issue had been one of national independence. Yugoslav communists whilst copying Soviet institutions had insisted on their right to run their state according to their own interpretation of Marxist-Leninism, adapted to conditions in Yugoslavia and in the interests of the Yugoslav people. They denied that the Soviet Communist Party was the final authority on interpretation of communist doctrine, that it had the right to interfere in the government of other communist states. They carried this argument further and denied

that there was only one correct way of putting Marxism into practice, pointing out that it had been evolved in the nineteenth century
when twentieth-century conditions were unknown; ultimately they
accused the Soviet Union of using communism as an instrument to
further its own national imperialistic aims.

The split remained complete until after the death of Stalin, and
when relations were gradually re-established, it was the Russians
who admitted they were wrong and took the initiative in *rapprochement*. Tito as spokesman of the Yugoslav Communist Party, has
never altered his position on the right to establish independent
national forms of communism. His successful stand destroyed the
Russian claim to total authority over world communism.

But in 1948 this result could not be foreseen. Soviet hostility put
the whole Titoist revolution in danger. Other communist states, with
varying degrees of enthusiasm (Polish communists had secret
sympathy for, Albania was bitterly against, Tito's line) supported
Russia; Yugoslavia had no friends in the West, and there was danger
that Russia might invade to overthrow Tito. This did not happen,
and may never have been contemplated, for it could easily have
precipitated a war with the West which even Stalin did not want at
that time. Few Yugoslav communists supported the Soviet line,
and most of these were gaoled. Yugoslav communists rallied behind
Tito; he was supported by the great majority of the Yugoslav people,
for non-communists saw that a Soviet controlled government
would be a much worse alternative. People and party were again,
as during the war, united in national opposition to a foreign danger.

The Cominform quarrel gave Yugoslav communists the opportunity to re-examine the theory and practice of their government
since 1945. They already knew that it had been unsuccessful in many
respects, and the break with Russia allowed them to reject Russian
practice which it had been heresy to criticize before. Change came
gradually, for admiration of Soviet communism had become in-
grained by years of indoctrination. In 1948 the first reactions of
Yugoslav leaders were to examine and try to refute the criticisms contained in the Soviet letters. The main criticism in home policy was
of insufficient communism – weak policy towards the peasants in

allowing them to keep their land and not enforcing collectivization, in treating them too mildly and favouring them at the expense of the workers; weakness in keeping the Communist Party as an almost secret organization, hiding it behind the Peoples' Front. It was pointed out that a Yugoslav Communist Party Congress had not been held since 1928. There was a host of other criticisms, many petty, personal and verging on comic opera – the Yugoslavs had dared to shadow Soviet agents, to counter their efforts to recruit Yugoslav spies; Yugoslav leaders were conceited and arrogant and Djilas had dared to say that the behaviour of Soviet officers in Yugoslavia had been inferior to that of British officers. All these criticisms were refuted point by point in the Yugoslav letters which also made their own counter-charges.

But some efforts were made to meet Soviet criticisms. A drive started against the peasants to force them into co-operative farms had disastrous results which will be described later. A congress (the fifth) of the Communist Party was hastily called in Belgrade in July 1948 at which a report of Party work since 1928 was delivered by Tito, and the quarrel with the Soviet Union was explained to Party delegates.[56] These measures failed to pacify the Soviet Union which demanded complete capitulation; other communist states were forced to join in economic sanctions against Yugoslavia. A Soviet call to Yugoslav communists to overthrow Tito's régime met with no success. All leading Yugoslav communists except one important war time leader, Arso Jovanović (shot whilst trying to leave the country), stood firmly behind Tito. Two other Yugoslav leaders, Hebrang and Žujović, together with a number of other 'Cominformists' were imprisoned. Some escaped abroad.

Since Tito had no intention of capitulating, the quarrel resulted in a complete break with Moscow. This set Yugoslav communists free to follow their own independent line, but they were dangerously isolated in a hostile world. Yugoslavia was eventually saved from this isolation because the Western allies, Great Britain, the United States and France, were prepared to give Yugoslavia economic aid rather than see it destroyed by Stalin. Aid came after 1951 but in the intervening years Tito had shown that he had sufficient national support to stand against Stalin, that the new Yugoslavia was not going to disintegrate under the pressure of Soviet displeasure and economic sanctions.

By 1951 it was evident that Tito had won the struggle against the Cominform. The state was sufficiently secure to allow a wholesale reorganization of government. The Stalinist system was scrapped and condemned as bureaucratic, a deeply derogatory adjective. It was officially admitted to have been inefficient, to have concentrated power in the hands of a few, yet to have led to a Parkinsonian increase in the numbers of petty officials who created work for them-selves. Decentralization of government was to be the solution, and from 1951 this was gradually introduced. In Belgrade a number of federal government departments were abolished; responsibility for executive government was given to the six republics. In local government the powerful executive committees and their political officers (*poverenici*) disappeared. Thousands of people at all levels of government had to find new jobs. (Federal employees declined from 43,500 in 1948 to 8,000 in 1955.)

The changed system of government was set out in 1953 in a 'New Fundamental Law' which replaced the 1946 constitution. The head of state and supreme commander of armed forces was to be a Presi-dent, elected by and responsible to the Federal Peoples' Assembly (Tito was duly elected). State executive powers rested with a Federal Executive Council also to be elected by, and responsible to the parliament. State secretaries were established for federal defence, internal affairs, national economy, budget and state administration. This meant a great reduction in government departments. The make-up of parliament, the Federal Peoples' Assembly, was drastically changed. The Council of Nationalities, with a representation re-duced from 215 to 70 (ten for each republic, six for the Vojvodina and four for Kosovo-Metohija) was merged into the Federal Council which was composed of deputies elected on the basis of one repre-sentative to 60,000 inhabitants.

The new feature of the Federal parliament was the introduction of a Council of Producers as the second chamber. Deputies for this were to be elected (by indirect voting through electoral colleges) by 'workers and employees of economic enterprises, members of agri/ cultural co/operatives, craftsmen and handicraft workers acting through craftsmens guilds'.[57] The two houses were to sit separately except for joint sessions for certain affairs such as the election of president and other officers. The work of the Chamber of Producers was stated to be in the 'fields of economy, work and social insurance' (article 40) – a vague definition which allowed for changes in interpretation. This pattern of government, with the exception of the president, and in smaller numbers, was repeated for parliaments in the republics. Chambers of Producers were also set up in all divisions of local government.

The Chambers of Producers were a Yugoslav invention, unique and not derived from any known constitution elsewhere – though the idea of additional representation for certain classes of citizens has been tried out in some other countries. The aim behind this experi/ ment – and it was admitted to be an experiment – was to strengthen the influence on government of the working class, the traditional ally, according to Marxist theory, of communist government. The Chambers of Producers were to be a safeguard against the develop/ ment of bureaucracy on the one hand, and the possibility of excessive influence on government of non/communists on the other. The invention was for ideological more than practical purposes.

The Chambers of Producers did not have a very successful history and were subjected to a number of amendments in succeeding years. Problems arose over the system of nomination and election of candi/ dates, over the definition of who was a worker (why were intellectuals to be excluded, should working wives of peasants who were mem/ bers of co/operatives have the vote?), and over the definition of functions. Deputies were to be people actually engaged in manual (widely interpreted) work; but as deputies they had little time for such work and became virtually disqualified. The Chambers of Producers did not 'take on'. Interest in nomination and election of candidates was often low, especially in country districts where peasants could not see how their interests were served by these chambers; in industrial areas and towns the workers' main interest was in the new Workers' Councils which had been established for each industry and occupation. When a new constitution was issued in 1963, the Chambers of Producers were not renewed.

A new feature of the 1952 constitution which had more success, was the reorganization of the communes to become a new unit of local government. Under the 1946 constitution communes had been small, less important than the village committees (later abolished except for specially remote areas where it was difficult for the communes to operate). Communes were now enlarged to include bigger groups of villages and hamlets. They averaged from 3,000 to 7,000 inhabitants instead of the earlier units of 2,000 people or less. They were to have two salaried full-time officials in addition to an elected, but paid, full-time working chairman of the Peoples' Committees.

After 1952, local government was at three levels – republican, district (srez) and commune. All still had their elected Peoples' Committees; the republic had overall responsibility for government and economic planning, and its institutions were a miniature of those of the state. The district government resembled in some ways local government in England; additional to the elected Peoples' Committees with their full-time chairmen and secretaries, each district had a number of other committees (saveti) of elected or co-opted members – the latter were usually specialists in a certain field – public health and education for example. These committees, as in England, were the watch-dogs of the public on the activities of the permanent local officials of which an increasing number were appointed for each district, to look after finance, education, health, public services etc. Appointment of these officials was by the Peoples' Committees, and vacancies had to be publicly advertised.

A very important development brought about by the decentralization was that the districts (under the authority of the republics) were given responsibility for, and a financial share in the whole economic activity of the area they covered. They could claim a share in the profits of factories and works to provide revenue for local government which could also be increased by local taxes (the equivalent of rates in England) and by charging fees for certain services. Districts provided the revenue necessary for the communes. With the exception that the Councils of Producers at all levels were abolished in 1963, this system of local government has remained in being to the present. The recent tendency has been to increase the powers and responsibilities of the communes.

What effect did these changes have on the lives of ordinary people? They certainly improved efficiency and liberated initiative and interest to improve local conditions and develop resources at every level from the republic to the village. They also brought many more people to play a part in local government; it has been calculated that in Croatia one in a hundred people had to sit on some govern-ment committee; today in most of the country the ratio is even less.

Yugoslavia had still a predominantly peasant population. Peasants who were not communists (as many ex-Partisans tended to be) had been bitterly disillusioned by the government's policy since 1945; many disliked the communists and retained the traditional Balkan peasant hostility to government and townspeople; the 'we' and 'they' of the pre-war years. The 1953 reforms aimed to break this antithesis by bringing more people into public life. On the whole, it may be said to have had some success, but it is naturally a slow process.

The Yugoslav leader's most important aim was still to protect the revolution, keep power in the hands of the Communist Party (which in 1952 changed its name to League of Communists); but changed methods were required. Communists now had to make more effort to hold their place in public life; the system was still loaded in their favour since they continued to be the only political party. In all elections voters now had to have a choice of candidates; but choice was only between personalities, for opponents of the government could still be excluded. In political life, the government could now, as it could not in the Stalinist period, be criticized – up to a point. But it was not permitted to oppose basic communist conceptions of government and economic development.

In these conditions the communists managed to hold their own. The previous communist leaders still held all important government positions; a year after the reforms, a third of the elected members of Peoples' Committees in communes were communists, about a half in districts, and about 90 per cent in cities (of which there were now twenty-two). It would be a mistake to assume that in local – or central – government the aims and work of communists were all disliked by the general non-communist majority of Yugoslavs. Peoples' Committees (as many independent observers of their work testify), were usually inspired by local pride, strongly devoted to local interests which they sometimes pursued in opposition to republican or national policies. Under the new system, though institutions were different, and the proportion of population taking part greater, the work was in many ways very similar to that undertaken in local government in any country of comparable size.[58]

The 1953 constitution also provided for a reform of judicial procedure which was amplified by new laws in 1954. More important than new machinery was the spirit in which it was used. This became more judicial, less subject to political considerations; above all many aspects of the police state – spies, informers, political imprisonments and intolerable restrictions on the individual freedoms, which the constitution had guaranteed but the State denied during the Stalinist period – gradually decreased or disappeared. Numbers of political prisoners dropped from 52,506 in 1949 (official figures) to 36,146 in 1950, 22,359 in 1951 and 15,484 in 1952. By 1964, they averaged 1·2 per cent of a total of 16,250 persons serving prison sentences.[59] The political atmosphere in the country remained very sensitive, especially in reaction to the different phases in the cold war, for Yugoslavia's exposed position between East and West both geographically and ideologically, was uniquely vulnerable. Yet from the point of view of all Yugoslavs in town and country, communist or non-communist, conditions improved from 1950 and especially in the latter half of the fifties and early sixties.

The development of liberalized government did not take place in a vacuum and it was greatly aided by the slow but steady improvement in economic conditions. Improved relations with the West came with economic aid given to prevent Yugoslavia falling into the power of Soviet Russia after the Cominform break. *Détente* with the West brought a compromise settlement of the Trieste problem in 1954; Yugoslavia retained Zone B, Italy Zone A including the port of Trieste. A Balkan Pact with Greece and Turkey (1953) gave Yugoslavia some security against the continued hostility of her Cominform neighbours, of whom Albania especially remained virulently hostile. In the United Nations, Yugoslavia (elected a member of the Security Council in 1949) began to play an active part among the uncommitted nations – those who would give wholehearted support neither to East nor West. Tito's international prestige had been enhanced and this was recognized by invitations to visit many countries including England and France and eventually in 1963 the United States and some South American countries.

Yugoslavia had emerged from the Cominform quarrel politically and economically stronger, more independent, possibly more united as a nation. The Soviet leaders, with Stalin dead and his tyranny admitted, acknowledged that they had been at fault. Krushchev himself (with Soviet Party Chairman Bulganin) visited Belgrade in 1955 to make peace. This was not easily done, for Yugoslav leaders were naturally suspicious of Soviet overtures and determined not to cede any part of their national independence. They were also by this time launched enthusiastically on the theoretical justification of their 'new road to socialism', their national form of communism which has been called Titoism. This aggressive independence was not what Soviet leaders had expected, and relations between the two countries remained cool until after 1960. By 1963 Chinese communist hostility to Russia had come into the open, shattering again, and perhaps for good, the monolithic conception of world communism under Russian leadership. Although many motives of the Chinese communists seemed to Western eyes to be analogous to those of the Yugoslavs, there was no *rapprochement* between China and Yugoslavia. Chinese communists violently denounced Titoism and eventually linked Yugoslavia with Russia as heretics to true Marxist-Leninism. In these circumstances Russia needed Yugoslav support in preventing other communist parties being suborned by China. Yugoslav leaders were now able to negotiate on terms of equality with the Russians – a position they had continually demanded, but never enjoyed before. Yugoslavia and Russia drew closer together;

economic and cultural agreements were signed (1962 and 1963) and friendly relations cautiously resumed.

By 1963 Yugoslav leaders had decided that ten years successful development of the state had made the 1953 constitution out of date. Increased industrialization had brought important changes in the structures of society, the 'socialization' of the economy had developed. After an adequate period of trial some of the 1953 institutions had been found unsatisfactory. Decentralization in practice had often gone too far, Chambers of Producers had not proved a success. Workers' Councils and communes on the other hand had been generally successful and experience had shown what changes were needed in political and economic institutions.

A new constitution was adopted in June 1963. This constitution contains many of the basic principles which had characterized previous constitutions – the federal character of the state, autonomy of the six republics, definitions of the freedoms, rights and duties of citizens, and, with some changes, of the fields of operation of the law and organization of law-courts etc.[60] But this constitution also made much more detailed definitions of the institutions of local government – of the communes, the districts as well as the republics (Chapter 5) – than had appeared in previous constitutions. It incorporated the changes introduced by law and decree that have already been described as having taken place in the previous ten years of liberalization of government. It also incorporated (Chapter 2) the institutions that had been introduced into economic life, the principle of 'socially owned means of labour, and self-management of the working people in production and distribution of the social product' and the institutions of Workers' Councils and co-operatives. Article 23 stated that citizens shall have the right 'of ownership to objects for personal consumption and use or for the satisfaction of cultural and other personal needs, of ownership of dwelling houses and dwellings for their personal and family needs'; but added that limits to such ownership shall be determined by law.

One innovation of this constitution was in the character of the Federal Assembly, to be composed of delegates elected by communes and republics. There were to be four other chambers, for Economic Affairs, Education and Culture, Social Welfare and Health and Organization – a political chamber for delegates of the working people.

Each was to have 120 deputies elected in the ratio of one member to an equal number of inhabitants so that one or several communes as a constituency should elect one member to each chamber. Election to the Federal Assembly was to be by direct suffrage, to the different chambers by communal assemblies acting as voting colleges. Names of candidates to be voted on could be drawn up by meetings of the electorate, groups of citizens, or at meetings of 'working communities', and every citizen with the right to vote (over eighteen years) was to be eligible for election. Deputies could be recalled at any time if a majority of the electorate voted for their recall.[61] No deputy or officer of the state could serve in the same position for more than two consecutive terms.

This constitution abolished the Councils of Producers which had aimed to give extra political power to industrial workers and people in all walks of life whose association with socialist institutions such as co-operatives showed support for the basic ideas of the Communist Party. The intention had been to weaken the influence in elections of private peasants and other self-employed people who still existed in large numbers, and whose support of the official form of socialism could not be taken for granted. The same aim was clearly present in the new constitution but a more positive principle is evident. This is the attempt to enforce participation of large numbers of people in their own government. The principle that deputies and federal officers (except Tito) may not serve in the same position for more than two consecutive terms is applied throughout the whole system of republican and local government. The intention is to bring about participation of more people in the responsibilities of government;[62] it also aims to provide safeguards against power being concentrated in the hands of a few people.

The system differs greatly from parliamentary democracy as understood and practised in Great Britain which, it should be emphasized, the Yugoslavs have never experienced; but it also differs greatly from

123

communist government in other communist states. In Yugoslavia many people besides communists must take part in government. The leaders hope that this will educate the people in the practice of their conception of socialist democracy by giving them practical experience of government leading to approval by association. Yugoslav political theorists claim that the 1963 constitution is a new stage in the process of 'withering away of the state' of classical Marxist theory; that the constitution provides for the withering away of central authority and the transfer of power to organs of social self-government (in communes and other local government and to Workers' Councils in the economic field). Thus the powers of the new federal government are limited to affairs of common interest to all republics – defence, security, uniform bases for political and economic life, protection of special development for underdeveloped areas etc. leaving most executive government in the hands of locally elected committees. The whole system is to have the support of the rule of law 'an integral part of, and prerequisite for socialist democracy, in addition to its being a safeguard against abuse, bureaucracy and arbitrary acts by individuals'.[63] The aims of the 1963 constitution are more complex than those of earlier constitutions. It aims to produce and protect a more advanced stage of 'socialist democracy'; to satisfy citizens both as individuals and as members of a particular republic (as Serbs, Croats etc); at the same time it aims to protect the leading role (power) of the League of Communists. The communist revolution is to continue in spite of devolution of authority.

ЖИВЕО 27 МАРТ ДАН БОРБЕ
ПРОТИВ ФАШИСТИЧКОГ ЗАВОЈЕВАЧА

27
МАРТ

БОЉЕ ГРОБ НЕГО РОБ

52 On 27 March 1945 Yugoslavia celebrated the ending of the Second World War.

53 Tito signed the document which proclaimed the Federal Peoples' Republic of Yugoslavia in November 1945.

54 The new republic accepted the USSR as the authoritative leader of communism. President Tito is seen here with Josef Stalin and Mr Molotov (Russia's Foreign Minister) at Moscow in 1946.

55 Dr Dragoljub Jovanović led the Yugoslav Opposition Party and was imprisoned in 1946 for criticizing government policy.

56 (*Below*) As a result of the Italian Peace Treaty of 1947 the Yugoslavs took over land formerly occupied by Italy. But the struggle over Zone B (the region claimed by Yugoslavia and Italy after the war) was not completely settled until 1953.

57 An Italian farmer moves his possessions to an area under Italian control whilst American troops prepare for the new division of territory.

58 In 1947 Yugoslavia launched a Five Year Plan with the help and support of the Soviet Union. This aimed at rapid rebuilding and industrialization. Belgrade was rebuilt by volunteers.

59 The effects of the raids of the Second World War were evident at Podgorica which later became known as Titograd.

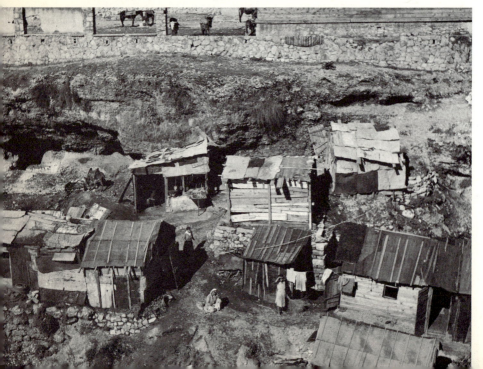

60 In 1948 Yugoslavia was expelled from the Cominform. It was with help of further western aid from 1950 that she was able to develop her many industries. A team of miners at the lead mine at Šuplja Stijena.

61 The excavation of the copper mine at Majdanpek was one of the many developments which had an important influence on Yugoslav economy.

62 The hydro-electricity industry was modernized. This power station is at Jajce.

63 This plant at Fala on the river Drava was built in 1918 but in order to increase the potential of the river a further plant was developed at Dravograd in this post-war period.

64 The large electro-industrial 'Rade Končar' factory at Zagreb was established as early as 1945.

65 One of the key projects of the first Five Year Plan was the development of the iron and steel industry which was not completed until 1956. This is the ironworks at Jesenice in Slovenia.

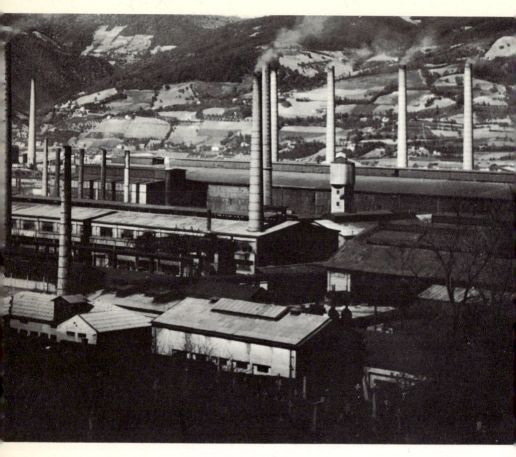

66 The steelworks at Zenica in Bosnia-Hercegovina.

5 Economic Planning and Industrial Revolution

THE MOST SPECTACULAR and far reaching changes in the new Yugoslavia have been brought about by an industrial revolution, planned and carried out by Tito's régime in the short space of twenty years. Before the war and in 1945, as has been shown in earlier chapters, Yugoslavia was backward, with a standard of living one of the lowest in Europe. Its resources were unexploited, its town dwellers few but privileged, its peasants for the most part poor, undernourished, politically impotent and living in archaic conditions.

By 1964, Yugoslavia was well on the way to becoming a modern, industrialized country. Industrial production was five times greater, and of an incomparably higher standard than in 1939. The few pre-war industries had been modernized and extended (the Zenica steelworks in Bosnia was only one example among many), new industries had been created in all parts of the country. New factories, blocks of flats, schools and public buildings were to be seen everywhere; even many peasants had new houses and farm buildings. Only half the population (which had increased at a rate of about 1·4 per cent per annum to over 19 million in 1964) was now engaged in agriculture, and the numbers of townspeople and towns had greatly increased. Some republics, especially Macedonia and Montenegro, still remained underdeveloped, and some remote parts of the country in most republics showed little surface change. But in general the industrial revolution changed a way of life and the changes could be seen in the appearance of the countryside and in the clothes and habits of the people.

To achieve this result in such a short time the Yugoslav people were forced to work hard and for a time to sacrifice their standard of living. Successful industrialization required a high investment of Yugoslav resources; it could not have been done without consider' able foreign aid which Yugoslavia was fortunate in receiving from the West after Tito's break with Russia. The history of Yugoslavia's economic development and industrialization in these years was full of difficulties, set'backs, mistakes and changed policies, but in the end it was a success story.

The need for economic planning was a firmly held communist belief and the first Federal Planning Commission began work in 1946 in the period when the Soviet example was still sacrosanct. A five year plan for the Development of National Economy 1947–51 was approved by the parliament April 1947.[64] Its ambitious aim was to industrialize the backward and largely agrarian country in five years; during this period national income was to be doubled, industrial output to be raised to five times the 1939 level. Simul' taneously social services were to be improved, agricultural production increased, and the standard of living (judged by consumption of food and goods) raised. The plan did not propose large investment into agriculture. Many people both in and outside Yugoslavia at the time criticized the plan as over'ambitious, patently unrealizable. Yugoslav leaders and planners were impatient of such criticism. This is one of the cases where the euphoria of war'time success prob' ably clouded their vision; they believed that the success against all odds in wartime could be repeated. Ignorance and inexperience in the highly technical field of economic planning was fortified by ideological intransigeance. Yugoslav leaders went ahead regardless of, and greatly irritated by, adverse criticism.

The money required to set up new industries was to be provided by investment of a high proportion (28 per cent) of the total esti' mated national income over the five year period. The Soviet Union (in spite of disapproval of the plan) agreed to a credit of $135 million for machinery and equipment for new industries. Equipment was

134

to come from industrialized states of the Eastern bloc – Czechoslovakia and Poland. Joint SovietYugoslav air and river transport companies were to be set up.

Planning and administration were centralized in Belgrade. Federal plans were drawn up for each year, and republican plans had to be coordinated with them. In Belgrade economic ministries for groups of commodities decided how much should be produced, how much consumed, during the year; republics, factories and enterprises were given their production quotas which were calculated (and had to be reported on), per week, per day and sometimes per worker. Conditions of work, credit, costing, distribution, prices – everything was worked out in advance. Since all industry was owned by the state and all finance came from the National Bank, financial transactions between one state enterprise and another were simply book transfers. Credit was cheap, easy to obtain; all profits accrued to the state and losses were borne by it. It left nothing to republican, local or individual initiative. Workers and enterprises were encouraged to 'exceed their norms' i.e., produce more than their quota; shock workers received bonuses, but wages were kept low.

The system did not work. Excessive centralization led to irresponsible waste of state assets. No proper provision had been made for amortization. Serious mistakes had been made in planning amounts and kinds of goods needed for the home market – some items, needles, combs, razor blades for example had been omitted, but hats and slippers of inferior quality which none would buy flooded the market. Marketing was separated from production, the system of distribution was chaotic, bedevilled by poor communications, inexperience and an inefficient zoning system. There were gluts in some places, scarcity in others. A major difficulty was lack of adequate manpower. In spite of unemployment in agricultural areas, industry and administration lacked trained, even educated workers. There was surprisingly no direction of labour; Belgrade tended to attract the able administrators, enterprises competed as best they could for the very few expert and trained personnel, and the turnover of labour was very high. There was a staggering increase in officials and paperwork (each enterprise had to submit between 600 and 800 reports each year).

Production was also affected by the political conditions of the police state and by the very difficult conditions of ordinary life. There was an acute housing shortage, and a food rationing system, though designed to help the industrial worker, did not always work. Basic foods were supplied against a ration card, and the food stocks for this were supposed to come from government purchases from the peasants. Additional food could be bought from peasants who were allowed to sell on a 'free' – i.e., not state controlled – market. But peasants did not co-operate with this scheme, and almost everybody had to supplement rations by buying food at high prices on the free market. Low wages made no provision for this. Many workers had to do two jobs.

An important factor in the money-goods relationship in these years was remittances sent by Yugoslav émigrés living abroad. These consisted of parcels of food and high-quality consumer goods. Between 1946 and 1951 their value totalled $123·9 million. These goods were resold, often repeatedly in state second-hand shops (charging 5 per cent commission) or illegally on the black market. Until after 1951 they were the only high-class consumer goods on sale.

In spite of these difficulties some results were achieved. National income increased a little (1·9 per cent per annum), industrial production rose (6·4 per cent annually), transport improved. Above all, these years were rich in experience. Final assessment of the Five Year Plan can never be made because the break with Russia in 1948 and Russia's economic blockade forced the modification and final abandonment of the plan as originally conceived. Soviet and other communist states' deliveries of raw materials, machinery, and equipment for projected new industries dwindled to a stop in 1948-9. By 1950 industrial output had ceased to expand and in 1951 it declined. Russia's threat to the régime and to Yugoslavia's independence as a state meant that much industrial effort had to be switched to a rapid build-up for armaments industries. The labour force and many aspects of civilian life were disrupted by the need to maintain a large army and security forces.

During 1950 it became apparent that the political crisis was passing. By this time Yugoslav leaders had had time for critical examination of the Soviet-inspired system of government and its effects in political and economic life. They concluded that the whole system tended to defeat its own aims. New ideas were being evolved leading to a changed and much less rigid approach to economic planning. Basic ideas behind these changes were the same for economic as for political life. Centralization and exercise of power from above had been proved inefficient, it was now thought to be morally wrong and not in keeping with a correct interpretation of Marxist-Leninism. The state as the expression of the will of the people must allow the people as individuals to take full and responsible part in its institutions.

In economic life the new institutions were to be Chambers of Producers, already mentioned, and more important the introduction of a new system of workers' self-management of factories (and almost all other forms of work) through elected Workers' Councils. A law transferring ownership of state enterprises to the workers as representatives of society was introduced on 26 June 1950. Workers' Councils were to play a very important part in Yugoslav economic life and were subjected to a number of changes in their powers and function. These are described in more detail below.

In 1950 a need as urgent as the creation of new institutions was how to raise funds to keep industry going and provide food to avert nation-wide starvation. The harvest of 1950 was disastrous, hit by drought and badly affected by passive resistance of the peasants reacting against the government's collectivization policy which had been intensified after Soviet criticism. Yugoslavia was saved from a really critical economic situation by aid from the West.

British aid 'to keep Tito afloat' and prevent starvation was first given in small quantities of food shipments in 1950; aid from the United States and (to a much less extent) from France followed. Opposition to aid, especially strong in the United States, considered that it was helping to build up a communist state. Others considered aid as a realistic measure to keep Russia out of this vital strategic region of western Europe. Some people even at that time realized the importance of Tito's stand as an example to other communist states, and also believed that improved economic conditions might modify the character of Yugoslav communism.

Yugoslav leaders themselves did nothing to encourage such ideas. In post-war years they had been very cold – often abusive – towards the West. When they negotiated aid they made no startling volte-face and stipulated that they would accept no political strings, allow no interference in their internal policy.

By 1951 Britain had granted $29 million to be spent on food and raw materials, the United States had given $87 million for food. A second drought in 1952 meant that aid in food would have to be continued, and it was clear that unless the Yugoslav economy could be given the means for developing and improving, aid to Yugoslavia might become a permanency. Economic missions from the United States, Great Britain and France began to consider with the Yugoslavs what measures were necessary to make the economy viable.

In the following ten years Yugoslavia received from the United States $2,396·9 million worth of aid (in grants, credits and loans) for economic and military assistance. Of this $693·9 million was for defence. Britain's contribution was smaller, $120·4 million (£43 million) of which $54·3 million (£19·4) was in grants, the rest in the form of loans. France gave token aid. In 1962 the British government agreed to a financial guarantee of a £28 million loan to be raised privately.

In practical terms the aid affected every part of Yugoslav economy. Apart from military aid, it came in the form of food – wheat was imported from the United States every year – of agricultural items, including breeding stock, fertilizers, tractors, and other farm machinery and eventually equipment for agricultural industries such as canning factories and freezing plants. The aim was to build up agriculture so that Yugoslavia could export sizeable quantities of the kinds of foods that would be bought in the West, and at the same time produce enough to feed her own population. Much aid was spent on imported raw materials – oil, hard coal, wool and cotton for the textile industries etc. This released Yugoslav funds to buy equipment for industry. Where aid was used for purchase of equip/ ment for specific industries, it had usually to be justified to the Western economic missions by showing that the projects were feasible. An important part of aid was spent on training Yugoslav technicians (of almost all kinds; specialists for agriculture, industry, medicine, social services and in many other fields too numerous to list); some went abroad to be trained, to Britain, the United States, Italy, Germany, Denmark for example, others learnt from experts sent from these countries to Yugoslavia.

Western aid enabled Yugoslavia to carry through the industrial revolution that had been the object of the abortive Five Year Plan. It helped to stabilize Tito's régime, to restore friendly relations with the West, and through the many necessary contacts, to remove the iron curtain of mutual disapproval, ignorance and misunderstanding that had separated her from the West after 1945. Trade had to be reorientated to Western, later to all other non/communist countries. Yugoslavia began to be interested in the economic organizations of European states as well as those of all United Nations agencies.

All these contacts influenced Yugoslav economic thinking and practice. It is unlikely that they changed any fundamental com/ munist aims. Had Western expert advice been accepted in 1952, industrialization would have been drastically scaled down in favour of heavy investment into agriculture. Instead, Yugoslav leaders insisted on going ahead with development of industry, but they had to cut down the programme of the Five Year Plan to a limited number of key projects selected from those begun in 1947; the choice of these was significant, for they included development and modern/ ization of the steel industry, of coal, iron, copper, lead/zinc mines and other industries for metals and minerals; they included power industries – oil extraction and refinery, hydro/electric power. Bauxite and aluminium production were also included and chemical, textile and timber industries. These clearly indicated a country developing its heavy industrial potential. Many key projects were finished by 1953 though the whole programme was not completed until 1956. A new system of economic planning was being intro/ duced from 1952 onwards, simultaneously with the decentralization and reorganization of political life, but rapid industrial development remained the major economic objective.

New ideas on economic planning and organization of economic life brought tremendous changes. Detailed state planning and powers to put federal plans into effect were abandoned, the market was freed from most controls, free play was allowed for supply and demand to determine flow of goods as in capitalist economies. Enterprises could decide what to produce, how much to charge, how to distribute goods, and in most cases planned their own exports.

The Federal Planning Commission was stripped of its executive and administrative powers and replaced by a small, technical Federal Planning Institute, whose work was to draft general economic plans, both long and short-term and present them for consideration first to the Federal Executive Council, then to committees of the federal parliament, and finally after public discussion to parliament. The Planning Institute had no powers to see that its plans were put into effect. It was left to the discretion of republics – with their districts and communes, all of which had their own planning authorities to carry out the general aims of the plans in their own ways.

Republican planning institutes (with sections for heavy and light industry, agriculture and forestry, finance and administration) were responsible only to the republics' parliaments. Federal, republican and local plans could be modified either during the planning stage or when being put into execution; the whole system was designed to be fluid and practical. A federal plan for each year had to be accepted by the full federal parliament, and this took the place of an annual budget; it allocated the distribution of federal investment funds, and gave a forecast of national revenue and expenditure.

In theory it would have been possible for republics to thwart the major objectives of federal planning. To avoid this, much effort had to be put into consultation, co-ordination and co-operation between the various levels of planning. Political watch kept over nomination of deputies for Peoples' Committees and republican parliaments also helped to prevent local plans running counter to official aims.

Annual allocation of federal investment funds and the increasingly strict control over the way in which Workers' Councils disposed of the funds of individual enterprises also helped to control local planning.

Certain matters vital to national interest remained under federal control, amongst these were defence, railways, electric power in regional or national grid, and responsibility for seeing that the more underdeveloped republics received extra federal help, which in effect had to be subsidized by the more highly developed republics, Croatia and Slovenia. In spite of all this, many people in the late nineteen-fifties felt that economic decentralization had gone too far.

Between 1952 and 1956 whilst key projects in heavy industry were being completed, there were only annual plans. A second Five Year Plan, very different from the earlier 1947 one, was issued for 1957-61. In a short text, it outlined the main economic problems – short-age of raw materials, of electric power, of agricultural produce and consumer goods. Since many of these things still had to be imported in large quantities there was a large deficit in the balance of payments (total value of imports exceeded that of exports). The general aim was to find means of producing more, especially more food and consumer goods so that imports of these could be cut down, and yet make provision for the general standard of living to improve steadily. At last the immediate needs of ordinary people were to be catered for – the crying need for good quality household goods, clothes (not utility garments of Soviet pattern, but good quality clothes of European standard), even luxuries such as cosmetics, washing machines, refrigerators, television sets; all these, though not specifically provided for, were made possible by this Second Five Year Plan.

Part two gave statistical estimates for production in various sectors of the economy; the Gross Social Product[65] was to increase by 57·6 per cent over the five years, with an average annual rise of 9·5 per cent. National income was to increase by similar percentages. Detailed figures were given for each of the sectors into which Social Product is divided; industry was to increase annually by 11 per cent, construction by 10·9 per cent, transport by 9·1 per cent and agriculture by 7·4 per cent. Although this last figure was smaller than for production in industry, it represented in fact a big change in policy, for agricultural production, which had been neglected for so long, could not be raised at all without a big increase in investment (scheduled to rise by 195 per cent, over the whole period). It was believed that as newly built, or recently equipped industries were coming into production all the time, investment into industry would only need to rise by 11·9 per cent, and most of this was to go, not to heavy industry, which had received the lion's share of investment previously, but to industries which produced goods for export (such as tourism, food-canning, wine, etc.) or those which produced goods which could be sold on the home market instead of being imported from abroad – for example, artificial fertilizers, farm machinery, bicycles, even cars. In those sectors not included in the Gross Social Product, especially in social services, estimates were made for a big increase in expenditure – in housing, schools and other community services (by 71 per cent or 11·5 per cent average per annum).

These rather arid figures are very important, for they explain why there was such a striking change in material conditions of life in Yugoslavia at the end of the decade. The plan was fulfilled (a year early), goods did appear in the shops, there was more food, housing improved a little. The purchasing power of wages, and the quantity and quality of things that could be bought improved, and Yugoslavs began to spend more and settle into a semblance of normal – if not luxurious – life.

A further Five Year Plan was issued for 1961–5; its aims and estimates of annual increases in the various sectors of the Social Product were not greatly different from those of the previous plan. The deficit in the balance of trade had not decreased in the previous five years as much as had been hoped for (many world prices had increased making imports dearer than estimated); again the aim was to increase exports, cut down on imports by substituting home-made products, and encourage anything that would earn foreign currency.

Between 1957 and 1961 Yugoslav exports were double those of the previous five years; imports rose less, by only 80 per cent. Both were affected by the bad harvests of 1960 and 1961. After 1955 Yugoslavia began to trade again with eastern Europe and Soviet

Russia; other trading links had been developed with the Middle and Far East. Trade became more diversified, organized on a world-wide basis, and western Europe, though still important was declining both as a supplier and as a market. Invisible receipts – especially from tourism – were trebled. By 1961 Yugoslavia's total foreign indebtedness had risen to $680 million, and servicing charges (payment of interest) on this debt were $70 million annually.[66]

Thus from every point of view; it was necessary for the productivity of the Yugoslav economy to rise. An overall 'perspective' plan was prepared by the Federal Planning Institute for the period 1960–80. One important feature was the provision of funds (loans and grants) for development of the more backward parts of the country, especially Macedonia and Montenegro. The planners had already made ten year (1953–63) plans for both industry and agriculture. By 1964 the period of spectacular expansion in industry was ended. There was a marked recession in industrial development in 1961 and in 1962 with only slow improvement in 1963; many firms faced the problem of large stocks of unsold goods. By this time Yugoslav industry was no longer that of an underdeveloped state. Problems of economic growth, of inflation, recession, the need to find expanding export markets were the same as for other states of Europe. Successful industrialization had brought its problems as well as its advantages.

6 The Evolution of Workers' Councils

'WE ARE INDUSTRIALIZING our socialist country to make it richer, to make the unexploited wealth accessible to all citizens of our country, so that the people can make use of these riches. . . .'[67] Workers' Councils, established by law in 1950, were designed as a means of fulfilling this idealistic communist purpose. They were also to serve many practical purposes – enable workers to take a responsible part in management of industries which they, as members of the state, jointly owned, and to prevent a dichotomy and hence hostility developing between management and workers. Through serving on the Councils, workers were to become educated and experienced in the multifarious problems of management.[68] This it was hoped would produce industrial harmony and break the cultural barrier that in the past had separated qualified, educated managers from less educated, often ignorant workers whose skills and experience were limited to their own particular jobs. It was also hoped that it would lead to greater productivity, higher profits for community, enterprise[69] and individual. There was, too, a belief that if workers had a greater share of responsibilities and profits, they would recognize the benefits of the new Yugoslav socialism and become convinced members or supporters of the Communist Party.

The law has been amended but its main provisions are still operative.[70] It required workers in all state economic enterprises (in industry, communications, transport, trade, agriculture and forestry, municipal and federal employment) to elect a Workers' Council to be the supreme management authority in each works or unit of work.

Each Workers' Council was to elect an Executive Committee and the law provided for each enterprise to have an appointed director.

Voting for the Councils is by secret ballot of all workers. Lists of nominations can be drawn up by an existing Council, by the Trade Union branch of the enterprise, or by any other group which is 5 per cent of the total number of workers. Voters' meetings can co-ordinate or amalgamate lists. In a secret ballot votes may be cast for any combination of nominated people, they need not be for a whole list, and voters may even add to their ballot paper names that have not been nominated. Those who get the majority of votes are elected.

Workers' Councils have between 15 and 120 members (depending on the numbers of workers in the enterprise); if there are less than 30 workers, the whole personnel constitutes the Council. At first, elections were annual, since 1960 they are held every two years. The Council elects from among its members its own chairman, who may not be a member of the Executive Commitee. It is his responsibility to call meetings which should be held at least every six weeks, and nowadays are usually held once a month. Members of Councils (and Executives) receive no extra pay and must be working members of the enterprise. They may not serve for more than two terms in succession.

The Executive Committee (three to seventeen members) is elected by the Council. In theory, at least three-quarters of its members must be workers engaged in actual production, the rest can be technical or other personnel; they need not necessarily be members of the Council. It deals with executive work in all its aspects from drafting proposals for long-term and short-term planning, to all questions of personnel – hiring, firing, complaints, wages etc. The law states that its duty is to see 'that the enterprise is being run correctly'.[71] The Committee chooses its own chairman (sometimes referred to as President not to be confused with the Council's chairman) who may not be the director of the enterprise, and he, together with the directors, draws up the agenda for meetings. Decisions are taken by majority vote, and attendance of half the members constitutes a quorum.

The work of Executive Committees is not the same as that of a

Board of Directors in Britain; Yugoslav Executive Committees deal with so much detailed work that they have to have frequent meetings, usually three, sometimes more, in a week, and members can receive compensation if their wages are affected by time lost from work. The Committee is responsible to the Workers' Council, but workers who have serious complaints about its work or decisions, have the right to inform a higher authority – the local Peoples' Committee, or other councils (commune, district or republic) or organizations of the industry in question.

Each enterprise has its own director. The 1950 law did not stipulate how he was to be appointed, and for two years (1950–2) directors continued to be appointed by the state through federal or local government committees, as they had been under the old bureaucratic system. This method resulted in many unsuitable and unpopular appointments, often of men who were safe politically, but technically unqualified. Since 1952, directorships have to be publicly advertised, and appointment is made by a special committee composed of equal numbers of representatives from the Workers' Council and the Peoples' Committee of the local commune. Directors must be qualified, though qualifications vary greatly with the size and work of the enterprise. New regulations provided machinery for dismissal of unsatisfactory directors. The Workers' Council could appeal for dismissal to the local Peoples' Committee. If the Committee did not agree, a new Workers' Council had to be specially elected, and if this continued to support the demand for dismissal, the Peoples' Committee had to comply with the request. Only a small number of directors have been dismissed by this method. Since 1963 local Peoples' Committees have lost these powers, Workers' Councils now have the sole right to appoint and dismiss directors of their enterprises.

A director's duties were only briefly defined in the 1950 law but he was stated to be 'directly responsible for adherence to the laws, legal regulations and directives of the competent state organizations, and for assuring their application in the enterprise'. He was to be the legally accepted representative of the enterprise, could make decisions on employment of personnel, and 'undertake measures necessary for the fulfilment of the plan and for the correct management of the enterprise'.[72]

Thus both directors and Executive Committees had considerable powers over the actual running of their works or factory. In large enterprises and industrial combines – whose numbers increased with the rapid development and modernization of industry in the fifties and sixties – it was found necessary to evolve some kind of machinery for delegation of some of the many functions of management. Other Committees and Executive Councils for groups of factories were found necessary. Workers' Councils also had to delegate some work to committees and special sub-committees. In 1957 a law on labour relations made sub-committees for 'internal discipline' and the hiring and dismissal of labour obligatory for all Workers' Councils. In large works (such as Zenica with 10,000, Rade Končar with 5,000 workers) it was found that the Workers' Council itself could be out of touch with the needs and wishes of the workers it represented. Departmental Councils were the solution, elected in the same way as the Workers' Council (Rade Končar for instance has 11.) The foreman or head of the personnel in a department must attend its council's meeting. Departmental Councils did not take the place of, and were still responsible to the Workers' Council, but they provided an outlet for consideration of many matters that arose at shop-floor level, and allowed for more satisfactory discussion by smaller groups, of subjects on the agenda for Council meetings, so that Council representatives could know more about the wishes of the people they represented. These Departmental Councils did not replace, but sometimes overlapped the work of the Trade Unions.

It took some years before the system of workers' management could be organized so as to combine efficient management with freedom for workers to make decisions about the finances and operations of the industries in which they worked. Experience showed up weaknesses in the 1950 law. Many Workers' Councils remained ineffective, manipulated (often in the interests of efficiency) by directors, Executive Committees or local Peoples' Committees. Although in early years the amount of profit which Workers' Councils could freely dispose of was small, it was not always used in a responsible way. Unsupervised, inexperienced, and without detailed instructions, Workers' Councils frequently made no provision in their accounts for depreciation, for accumulation of capital for investment. Many Councils spent all their freely disposable profits on extra wages, bonuses, holidays or sprees for the workers.

In 1954 new laws were introduced tightening control, especially financial control over the activities of Workers' Councils. They also extended the scope of the system to include every kind of economic enterprise in which labour was employed. Only self-employed people were exempted. Today Workers' Councils play a part in every kind of work, including schools, hospitals, civil service etc.

The new laws gave detailed instructions on how enterprises should distribute their income. Only income directly due to an increase in productivity could be used for social welfare or extra wages. Enterprises also had to take over social insurance payments (previously met by the state); it was made compulsory to set aside funds for depreciation. Detailed accounts had to be rendered both quarterly and annually to the National (later Communal) Bank.

New laws abolished the old rigid taxation system which had applied equally to all enterprises; its operation had subsidized inefficient firms at the expense of the efficient ones and it had not provided enough incentives for Councils to see that their firms forged ahead.

The 1954 laws introduced a new system of taxation. A tax previously levied on total wages paid by an enterprise, was abolished. An existing turn-over tax on sales of goods was retained as the basic indirect tax. Direct taxes were a 15 per cent tax on gross income which meant on the amount left over after certain specified costs had been deducted from total receipts. To encourage special industries some exemptions were made (food processing and mining for example). A further tax was on fixed assets – that is on the land, buildings, machinery, everything the enterprise used; this was considered as a form of rent to the state. Working capital was subject to this tax but not savings accumulated for further investment. This was in order to encourage enterprises to accumulate capital. Another tax designed as a kind of equalizer was levied (up to 40 per cent) on

148

an estimate of any extra revenue obtained through holding a monopoly. All these taxes had to be paid by the enterprise. In addition income tax was levied on earnings of all workers, employees, agricultural and other producers. A proportion of some of these taxes was assigned to local government authorities, but the greater part was to provide revenue for federal and republican expenditure.

Certain changes in these financial regulations were introduced in 1961. Their main object was to provide stronger incentives to enterprises to cut down costs, economize in manpower (which in many enterprises was underemployed), to invest in modern equipment and increase productivity. Individual income tax was replaced by a tax on the enterprise's gross income; there was also to be an excess profits tax when income exceeded 6 per cent of invested capital. Bigger allowances were made for replacement of machinery and capital equipment. The distinction between funds accumulated for investment and working capital was abolished. Enterprises had been inclined to accumulate capital (at a low tax), rather than spend it as working capital (subject to a higher tax). A flat rate of 4 per cent tax was imposed in the hope that enterprises would start to make more productive use of their savings. The interest to be paid on money borrowed from the State (republic or commune) was raised to stimulate enterprises to use their own capital (when state funds could be borrowed cheaply they had been tempted to use their own capital on social objects – clubs etc., or even lend their own capital out at a higher rate). By 1963 most enterprises were providing at least a third of new investment from their savings. One other change in 1961 was also designed to aid savings, this provided that communes were to receive taxes equivalent to 13 per cent of wage bills (less than they had received before) and 20 per cent of the amount allocated to investment funds – thus communes also would have an incentive to help enterprises to use their own savings for investments.

Although these financial regulations restricted the freedom of workers to dispose of the finances of their enterprises, other changes introduced during and since 1954 have given increased freedom of action in other fields. Workers' Councils are now completely free to decide what their enterprise shall produce and in what quantities.

They are free to sell (wholesale only, retail trading must be by special concerns) where they like, and with certain limitations, to fix their own prices.

Enterprises can compete with each other in the open market. When an enterprise wishes to increase its prices, it must apply, giving reasons, for permission to do so. If this is not refused within a speci/ fied time, the enterprise can go ahead. The state still fixes ceiling prices for certain items, especially where they affect the cost of living – e.g. rent, electricity and transport; it also guarantees minimum prices for agriculture. By this means it is able to encourage certain industries – as by a rise in the ceiling price in building industries in 1962 – and keep a permanent control over production.

Enterprises have been freed to engage in foreign trade. Up to 1961 this was not easy, for there was a complex system of trade restrictions designed to subsidize exports and restrict imports. A complicated exchange rate system helped to raise prices in Yugoslavia of imported luxury goods (e.g. motor/cars) and allowed some Yugoslav goods to be sold abroad at less than cost (and world) prices without any loss in profits to the enterprise. At the beginning of 1961 many of these controls were given up. A uniform rate of exchange (750 dinars to the dollar) and a Western customs tariff system were intro/ duced. This gave enterprises much more freedom to import goods and raw materials, though import prices went up by an average of 7 per cent and permission from the Federal Investment Bank still had to be obtained for import of equipment goods such as costly machinery.

In the matter of wages, enterprises also had a great deal of freedom. Minimum wage rates (to protect workers) were fixed by the state, but these were usually greatly exceeded by the wages actually offered, and enterprises competed with each other for skilled labour. In some of the less developed parts of the country very high rewards were offered to attract specially needed workers. Economic Councils for the various industries and local Peoples' Committees today take a part in assessing a recognized rate of pay in various types of work; but in the enterprise itself many other things are taken into account – different local conditions and aspects of work, efficiency, speed, group work etc., and these all affect wage rates.

Wages and salaries are no longer considered a cost of production. In accounting, they are deducted from the figure of income remaining after fixed charges (taxes, amortization, loan repayment etc.) have been paid; so that the greater the income of an enterprise, the more it can afford in wages. The law also provides that when an enterprise achieves a more favourable ratio of income to wages than the average for the previous two years, a part of the excess may be freely distri- buted by decision of the Worker's Council in wages or other benefits. Official policy has increasingly moved towards stimulating individual initiative by allowing Workers' Councils to distribute more of their income in the form of bonuses to wages.

Since 1954, the proportion of earnings which Workers' Councils could really control, and spend how they wished, has steadily, and recently rapidly, increased. In 1960 it averaged 20 per cent of the total income of enterprises; in 1961, this was nearly trebled to 55 per cent.

Another development introduced in 1961 resulted (as was intended) in spreading managerial responsibility more widely amongst the general body of workers. This was particularly impor- tant in enterprises with large numbers of workers. Enterprises were empowered to group workers into 'economic units' which were to correspond to a technical division of work – a workshop or depart- ment dealing with one aspect of work. They should be small enough for workers to know each other and their foremen, and understand the work of the unit. No definite size was stipulated, though numbers of about 40–80 workers were envisaged; enterprises were left to work these out for themselves depending on technical possibilities. In practice, economic units of anything from 5 to 300 have been established.[73] Management of the unit is the responsibility of an assembly of all workers which meets once a month. Larger units may also have an Executive Committee and sub-committees. These units were a further step in the government's policy of de- centralizing economic power and responsibility. They introduced the principle of direct self-government, in which all workers were to share as individuals and not only through elected representatives.

Development and effective use of economic units naturally varied from one enterprise to another but the purpose was to allow further opportunity for workers to discuss planning, overall management and current policy as it affected their own particular work. They could also put forward their views on the use of freely disposable funds. The unit provided both a preparatory forum for the meetings of Workers' Councils, and machinery for distribution and spending of funds at the disposal of the workers. In practice Workers' Councils have often allocated disposable funds to economic units to use as their workers decide best – as bonuses to wages, grants or loans for housing, supplements to insurance benefits, or for social club facilities.

Individual earnings, and the different questions connected with wage and salary scales have presented the Yugoslav government with many complex problems since 1945. Solutions have varied with the different theories and phases of economic planning. During the early bureaucratic period the Marxist principle of 'to each according to his need, from each according to his ability' was in operation. Workers were supposed to receive basic wages which would give them an equal share in the profits of their enterprise, regardless of the kind of work they did. The law set up wage-scales which varied a little according to level of skill and were uniform for all enterprises. Even the allowed differences tended to be levelled out by family allowances. The amount of work required from each worker was calculated. These were the 'norms'; workers who exceeded them received a reward – not always in money, more often a free holiday – and the most productive became 'shock workers' or peoples' heroes after the Soviet pattern. Emphasis was on work as a service to the community, a contribution to the building of socialism. The system was not a success; productivity of workers was low, they were not stimulated to greater efforts. Rigid egalitarianism prevented the flow of workers into jobs where they were most needed.

A new official attitude to wages and salaries came with decentralization after 1950. Two new principles were introduced, wage and salary scales were to be allowed a greater spread between maximum and minimum earnings, and money incentives were to encourage workers to do more productive, better quality work. Effective change came very slowly. In 1955 there was still only a small difference between wages received by skilled and unskilled workers,[74] even a manager only earned twice as much as an unskilled worker. 'The consequences were lack of responsibility, lack of initiative, lack of incentive'; only after this became obvious was a system for greater differentiation in wages and salaries introduced in 1957.[75] This divided workers' wages into two portions, the fixed (according to wage-scales agreed by the Workers' Council, Trade Union branch and local Peoples' Committee), and the variable, which depended on the profits of the enterprise and the amount available for free distribution in extra wages. This latter amount, as has been shown above, increased greatly in succeeding years with consequent big additions to wages and salaries. Enterprises began to compete with each other in offering higher basic wages to attract skilled workers who were in short supply either nationally or in a particular locality. In general the difference between wages for highly skilled and unskilled labour increased. Wages for the individual worker came to depend on the amount and quality or kind of work performed.

For a short time variable earnings were subjected to a graduated income tax (paid to the state) which aimed to cream off some of the excess earnings, but this was discontinued after 1959. Since 1961 further changes have been introduced to try to encourage workers to concentrate less on personal, more on group output. This has been the object of the distribution of variable wages through, and linked with, the joint output of the economic units.

It is very difficult to make comparisons between wage rates in Yugoslavia and other countries; a satisfactory conversion rate for currency has to be calculated, and there are many difficulties in assessing the purchasing power of money wages. In addition, wages in Yugoslavia only represent just over half of a worker's total income – most workmen also receive personal travelling and children's allowances as well as subsidized meals. They make no contribution to social insurance, which is paid by the enterprise, they pay no income tax, and wages are all 'take home' pay. Housing is scarce but rents are controlled and in spite of some permitted increase they are still subsidized by the government and well below the market price or level of rents in most other countries in Europe. Yugoslav workers often live in large family groups in which a number of adults are wage earners. This is why they have been able to buy the goods that have appeared in the shops since 1957 in increasing variety and quantity. Ten years ago, wages were below the minimum cost of living and many workers had additional jobs; today they are more adequate and where individual or group productive effort is successful, workers in industry can earn as much as highly skilled qualified professional people, as much as the top ranks of the civil service.

With so many institutions playing a part in regulating conditions of work – Workers' Councils, economic units, Peoples' Committees, not to mention Chambers of the various industries and Republican and Federal authorities – is there any function left for the Trade Unions in the Yugoslav economy? The answer is yes, but a different role from that of Trade Unions in Great Britain, the United States and many other capitalist countries. Since all Yugoslav industry, and most economic enterprises belong to the people there should in theory be no conflict of interests between management and labour. It is clear, however, that such conflicts can arise even in publicly owned industries in a socialist or communist state. In the past twenty years and especially since 1950, the Yugoslav leaders have shown a powerful determination to try to prevent the evolution of any organization that could represent the 'we' of the workers against 'they' of management. The aim of most of the organizational changes in economic life from 1950 to the present day has been to make workers identify themselves with management; even more to ensure that their interests are identical.

Fortunately for the Yugoslav leaders the Trade Union movement had no long history or strong following in Yugoslavia in 1945. Before the First World War, Trade Unions had had some success in Croatia and Slovenia; Tito had joined the Union of Metal Workers in 1910 a few days after he got his first job in a mechanic's workshop in Zagreb.[76] These Unions were weak, and agitation for improved wages and conditions mainly came from the left wing political parties – the Social Democratic parties and eventually the communists. In the Kingdom of Yugoslavia between the two wars, Unions were for a time proscribed and continued to be weak; industrial workers were few and funds were small. The government equated Trade Union activity with subversion and tried to suppress them. Different groups of workers were organized in separate Unions with local connections and regional loyalties so strong that they never formed a united national movement. They disintegrated during the Second World War with the deportation of industrial workers to Germany, and German control of Yugoslav industries.

Trade Unions were started again after the end of the war. They served a different and more limited purpose than before. As in all other aspects of economic life, a distinction has to be drawn between the Stalinist period before the break with the Cominform, and the decentralization and increasing liberalization that have taken place since. Between 1945 and the coming into operation of Workers' Councils in the fifties, workers had many industrial grievances which could have been handled by the Trade Unions had this been per-mitted. Had the many economic complaints been allowed to be directed into one channel it would certainly have become in effect a political party in the same way that the Labour Party grew out of the Trade Union movement in England. It could also have acted as a catalyst for regional complaints and rivalries. These were developments which Tito was determined to avoid. He was clear in his conviction that national unity could only be preserved if all opportunities for political or economic faction were forbidden. The Communist Party within the Peoples' Front was the only permitted political party and the Trade Unions became its support in industry. Their function was mostly to persuade workers to carry out govern-ment economic instructions. They undertook social work, building holiday homes and sanatoria, and were used to organize workers' education, especially in early years, basic education for literacy and elementary technical training.

After the introduction of the new economic policy, Trade Unions were able to undertake more work in protecting and furthering their members' interests. They still had to operate within the limits of laws and regulations controlling workers' self-management. But the system itself was less rigid, and the official aim was to get more workers to take part in management, to know and exercise their rights. This was a job for the Unions.

Looked at from a western point of view Yugoslav Trade Unions are in an ambivalent position. They have to accept official policy and most Union officials are communists. If they wish to make changes in industrial conditions they have to work through, not against official machinery. Thus Unions do not call official strikes. The right to strike is not forbidden by law, but until recently strikes were officially considered and treated as economic sabotage. Strikes have occurred, but the political pressure against striking is very heavy, and the official view is that in the new system of workers' management there are so many ways in which workers can seek and enforce redress of just grievances, that if a strike occurs, Union, Party, enterprise or local government representatives and officials have all failed to do their job properly. It means a local breakdown in economic management. Genuine grievances should be cleared up before they reach the build up that brings about a strike. Agitators are not tolerated; they can be brought before the courts as state enemies. The crux of the matter lies in what constitutes a genuine grievance, and how far workers' interests can be made identical with those both of the management and of the state.

The administrative machinery of the Trade Unions is similar to that of the state. The Confederation of (6 different) Trade Unions (total membership 2·7 million out of 9 million workers) has committees of elected representatives from each Union in all divisions of local government – republic, district and commune.[77] Its federal congress of delegates elects a Central Council (150 members who meet twice or three times a year) and is answerable to the Congress, but in between infrequent Congress meetings it wields considerable powers because its decisions are binding on all lower Union groups. The smaller executive of the Council is a Presidency, comprising presidents of all six Unions plus the president of the confederation organization in each of the six republics. The Presidency is the vital policy-making authority in the Trade Union organization. Its members are particularly concerned with all laws as they affect

156

workers, with federal policy, and with problems of co-ordinating activity in the different republics. A Secretariat of permanent officials does the routine work of administration.

Union membership is only strong among industrial workers; metal workers, miners, transport workers and builders for example. The total labour force in Yugoslavia is about nine million and of these over five million are agricultural workers, most of whom are self-employed. Backward conditions still present in many agricultural areas, the conservatism and individualism of peasants, their lack of tradition of organized labour, and suspicion of communist intentions help to explain why Union membership is only a small proportion of the total number of workers.

Workers' Councils and the system of workers' management have now been in effective operation for more than ten years. How have they worked out in practice? This is a very difficult question to answer. Assessments are often subjective and much depends on the point of view of the inquiry. Do the Yugoslav leaders think the experiment has succeeded in its purpose? How far are workers, and people in general, satisfied with this institution? Has it aided economic development and furthered democratic (i.e., share of the people in) government? Some answers can be given to these questions. It is also possible to indicate some of the complex material and varied observations on which people make their judgments. But conclusions must be tentative, for conditions in Yugoslavia still vary in regions and occupations from almost primitive to highly developed.

Some general conclusions can be made from statistics. Up to 1960 about 600,000 men and women had served on Workers' Councils; about 15 per cent of the total working population was serving on Councils or Executive Committees, and of these about 35 per cent were Communist Party (League of Communists) members. There were 11,000 Workers' Councils with a total of 214,306 elected members; members of Executive Committees totalled 68,000. In industry there is one Councillor for every seven or eight workers. In the past ten years one in every three or four workers has served a term as representative in some form of management – a high degree of participation.

How effective has this been? This is more difficult to decide, for proper assessment must depend on an intimate knowledge of the working (open as well as by devious manipulation) of Workers' Councils and Management Boards throughout the country. Visitors can see Workers' Councils in operation but it is often difficult – especially for foreign observers – to judge if what they see at any given time is representative for one particular industry, or for the Councils as a whole. Changes introduced by law, speeches of leaders and officials, articles in the press, and comments by individuals have also given many pointers especially to defects in the system – success is more intangible and not always so well publicized. In the past ten years, especially (but not only) at the beginning of the period, there were many criticisms of the effectiveness of Workers' Councils. It was reported that meetings were held less frequently than required by law; that agendas prepared by directors and Executive Committees controlled what could be discussed at Council meetings. Voting was said to be so frequently unanimous that it appeared that workers' representatives were too submissive to their executive. Many subjects brought before Councils were highly technical matters of planning and finance. Ordinary workers did not have the knowledge or experience necessary to question, criticize or suggest alternatives to the proposals. The same applied to members of Executive Committees and criticism has often been made that certain Directors controlled all effective decisions of their enterprises. Frequent press campaigns and President Tito during several speeches have criticized the 'omnipotence' of directors. At a Congress of Workers' Councils (the first) in June 1957 criticisms were made of the fact that many workers showed no interest in management, of the aloofness and apathy of many Workers' Councils, of a tendency even under this system for a division to develop between management and the general body of workers.[78]

These weaknesses would not be unnatural even in countries where industrial workers are more highly educated and have a longer period of experience behind them. They are often found in Trade Union institutions in Great Britain for example. With the historical background and existing conditions in Yugoslavia they were to be expected. They had in fact been anticipated when the scheme of workers' management was launched as far back as 1950. On that occasion, Tito stressed that workers' management could only become effective gradually.

Most of the official changes in the organization of workers' management have been directed to eliminating these weaknesses – the economic units, the greater control of Workers' Councils over appointment and dismissal of directors, increasing participation of Trade Unions and many provisions of the 1963 Constitution. The big increase in percentage of profits that Councils are allowed to distribute in wages and other benefits to workers (and its distribution through the small economic units) have also given workers more personal financial incentive to take an active part in running their enterprises. Much more interest is being shown as a result of these changes. Many examples could be quoted of very active Councils. It is probably true that these are increasing and the ineffective ones decreasing.

It will clearly be a long time before the majority of workers have the know-how to control many of the technical decisions that have to be taken in industry and other forms of work. Numbers of workers in industry have risen from 800,000 in 1953 to 1,140,000 in 1963 and are rising by about 7 per cent per annum. Between one and two per cent of these new workers entering industry each year are poorly educated peasants changing from agricultural occupations. There are many schemes for the education of workers (and most have some basic training in workers' management) including technical and general courses run by the enterprise or local Peoples' Committee. Workers' Universities have also been organized in all the republics. In 1963 there were 241 Workers' Universities with nearly 11,000 students. There is tremendous competition for places. Desire for education and training is very strong in all regions.

Yugoslav leaders themselves are convinced of the success of Workers' Councils. They are incorporated in the latest constitution and great claims are made for their political success. They are presented as the means of making democracy a reality for the individual. It is clear that as in other forms of democracy great vigilance is required to see that the system works properly; many of the changes introduced have been directed towards making sure that it leads to maximum economic growth. The rate of growth in Yugoslavia rose by 12·9 per cent between 1957 and 1960 compared with 2 per cent between 1949 and 1952. Although this is affected by many other factors, it seems certain that Workers' Councils have not hindered, and may well have helped, in promoting productivity. For ordinary Yugoslavs this means that they are associated with improved living conditions. Perhaps the only way to tell if workers are really satisfied with the system would be if Workers' Councils were taken away; no one doubts that this would now be very unpopular, at any rate as far as Workers' Councils in industry are concerned; in other occupations, especially those where the Council does not deal with distribution of profits, the system is perhaps not so well established. There will always be those in favour and those against self government in schools, civil service departments etc. The greatest danger in practical operation (as compared with stated aims) of workers' management is that it tends to create a new *élite*; but this is a danger in every changing society. For the present it can be said that the system has had sufficient success to have become an accepted institution unlikely to be abolished (though certainly subject to continual change and adaptation) as long as the present régime continues in power.

67 The progress of the first Five Year Plan was retarded by the break with the Soviet Union but the rebuilding of cities such as Titograd continued.

68 During these years Yugoslavia experienced set-backs and difficulties but today many modern towns are in evidence. A new block of flats at Titograd.

69 The contrast between the old and new at Sarajevo.

70 From the ruins of Belgrade a new town has risen.

71 The mining centre at Venenje.

72 A Yugoslav wine market outside Belgrade in 1953.

73 The Second Five Year Plan (1957–61) aimed at producing more food and consumer goods rather than importation from abroad.

74 Television sets are produced at this factory in Niš.

75 The refrigerator assembly hall at the 'Georgi Naumov' Factory in Bitolj, Macedonia.

76 The Workers' Councils enable workers to play a responsible part in the management of their industries.

77 There are many schemes for the education and training of workers. This is a training centre for young workers at the steelworks in Ravna, Slovenia.

78 Practical work at one of the industrial schools.

79 A class at the factory school centre in Tuzla, Bosnia-Hercegovina.

80 New living apartments for those employed at the copper mine in Majdanpek.

7   Trial and Error on the Land

PEASANTS, that is the people living and working on the land, have always in the past made up the great majority of the population of all South Slav lands. In the Kingdom of Yugoslavia, they were 76·5 per cent of total population; at the end of the Second World War they were 69 per cent, and today they represent only just over half the total population. Their numbers are declining as more peasants take jobs in industry and swell the numbers of people living in the rapidly developing towns. A new kind of peasant family has evolved since 1945 – the half peasants, those who gain part of their income from working in industry, part from working the land. In some families one or two members work in nearby industries whilst the women or other members work on the land; other peasants go into industry seasonally, so that agricultural work can be done at seed-time and harvest when it is most needed. As peasants have more contact with industry, their lives are changing very rapidly; age-old differences between townspeople and peasants are disappearing.

Before the Second World War, peasants living in different parts of Yugoslavia – in the rich valleys of Serbia or Croatia, the bare highlands of Dalmatia or Montenegro, in the wooded mountain slopes of Slovenia, Bosnia or Macedonia – had their own, often very archaic customs and ways of life. Peasants had more in common with each other than with the townspeople whom they regarded with a hostility which was heartily reciprocated. In the pre-1941 Kingdom there was a steady trickle of peasants who managed to get educated and become townspeople. Tito himself was one of these, and he has vividly described the process of transformation, the political education, the saving up for smart clothes, a diamond ring and presents to impress the family and villagers back home.[79] Tito became an artisan but many other peasants who went to the towns got jobs in commerce or government service. A few became very rich and these usually came to despise their origins. They had become 'gentlemen' and adopted the attitude of patronizing contempt with which townspeople regarded peasants.

Political conditions also contributed to the intensity with which peasants concentrated on their own ways of life. They remained attached to the land, deeply religious (of whatever faith), against all government, and very conservative. They preserved customs which had changed little in centuries. They had their own festivals, wore their own special clothes, homespun and embroidered in patterns indicating their local or group relationships. They had their own songs and dances, and preserved historical legend and traditions in heroic ballads.

All these things and the remote beauty of much of the Yugoslav countryside still exercised a powerful romantic appeal to Western travellers in the twentieth century as it had done in earlier times. But romantic appeal concealed a far different reality; for up to 1941 most peasants in Yugoslavia were poor, undernourished, subject to a high incidence of disease and infant mortality, ignorant, exploited, and without power to change their conditions.

Some mention of the changes which the Second World War brought for many peasants has already been made. As a result of food scarcity those who lived in the fertile food-producing regions were often able to eat better than the townspeople, and sell produce at high prices on the black market. They made high profits and could buy valuable articles – pianos, rugs, pictures, furniture, that townspeople were forced to sell to buy food. The role of peasants in relation to townspeople was reversed. They could exploit a sellers' market and it gave them a sense of power and taste for better living than they had ever had before.

Before the war, white (wheat) bread was not commonly eaten by peasants; wheat was sold for export and peasants ate maize or rye bread. Meat was not a regular item of diet, and sugar an expensive luxury. Since the war, they eat far more white bread, meat, sugar and butter than ever before. The sellers' market for all food (except perishable fruit in a bumper year) has remained ever since the war and has been a major problem for Tito's government. Since 1945 it has been only one of many intractable problems relating to peasants, land ownership and food production.

Official solutions for these problems have often fallen between at least two stools. Food production by the peasants has been vitally important to the success of government and of industrialization plans. Workers in industry, administrators and townspeople in general had to be fed. As food producers for the country and as the majority of the population, peasants had the whip hand. Marxist Leninism provided the theoretical answer to this situation. Karl Marx had held that the whole system of peasant agriculture was doomed; it was incompatible with progress in either capitalist or communist states. Communists had urged total expropriation of land and its exploitation for the state by means of armies of labourers. Agricultural labourers would thus become indistinguishable from their proletarian brothers in industry, the opposition between town and country would be eliminated. This theme, with a number of variations was incorporated in communist doctrine. The idea came to be accepted that private property in land could be abolished. When Stalin tried to do this in Russia he found such opposition that it had to be forced through with a brutality and loss of millions of lives that have now become notorious. Tito was in Russia during the thirties and knew what was going on. When he came to deal with the situation in Yugoslavia, he was not prepared to use such self-defeating ruthless methods. Moreover, conditions in Yugoslavia were different from those in Russia; a large part of Tito's support came from peasants, and from the beginning of his leadership, both from choice and necessity, Tito adapted Marxist theory to Yugoslav conditions. The Partisan programme issued during the war emphasized the inviolability of private property; but the precise meaning of this was left purposely vague, for it was vital at that time to get the support of the peasants.

After communists had attained power at the end of the war, policy had to be put into practice and this was when they came up against the restrictions of their own theories. In communist doctrine, workers were politically superior to peasants who owned private land and were therefore capitalists; rich – i.e. successful – peasants, contemptuously described as *kulaks*, were enemies of communist society. A communist government should not help private peasants to get rich by investing in agriculture; it should in any case first invest all possible resources into industry, for an industrialized country would be more powerful, have more communists and more prestige than a country made prosperous by the productivity of its peasants. As the communist government did get support from workers (who could in any case be more easily organized) it was not politic to allow peasants to become rich by selling food whilst workers' food was rationed and their wages low. A solution that would satisfy both need and theory was very difficult to find. This is not surprising since it has proved to be the most intractable problem in all communist countries. In Yugoslavia since the war, many solutions have been tried out and abandoned, with the result that until recently agricultural production has been poor and the situation of the peasants has been very unstable.

At the end of the war, Tito's general policy was to increase food production and 'socialize' agriculture. One immediate problem of providing peasants with seed, equipment and stock was dealt with by UNRRA which imported large quantities of agricultural supplies. Other urgent needs to regulate the land-holding system, provide land for the poorest peasants (many of them ex-Partisans) and resettle land abandoned by German owners at the end of the war, were dealt with by sweeping reforms. A Land Reform Law (22 August 1945) fixed maximum holdings at 45 hectares[80] of which only 25–35 hectares (depending on quality) could be cultivated land; Church property was limited to 10 hectares. Contrary to what is usually supposed, only a small amount of land – about 2 million acres – became available from holdings in excess of this maximum, and about half of this was forest or waste land.[81] Other pre-war land reforms had already broken up most of the large estates that had existed under earlier systems, in the South Slav lands.

The total amount of land made available by the 1945 reform was

3·95 million acres. About half of this land was retained by the state, and of this one half was forest land, the other half was used for state farms and other public institutions. Land sequestered from Germans amounted to 1,576,500 acres, mainly fertile land. 1,957,100 acres were allotted in smallholdings to 263,000 peasant families and 950,000 acres to 67,000 families who were moved to Vojvodina, Bačka and Slavonia from barren lands in Bosnia-Hercegovina, Lika in Croatia, Dalmatia, Montenegro and even from parts of Slovenia and Serbia.[82] One hundred and sixteen thousand acres of land given to these 'colonists' was assigned for co-operative or collective farms of which seventy-two were founded.

This resettlement of land did not get off to a very good start because everything needed for farm work was in short supply. In addition colonists who came from poor, often high mountain regions found it difficult to adapt themselves to the different ways of life and climate (they easily contracted tuberculosis and other diseases) of the Danube plain. But resettlement would have presented difficulties in any case, and in general much of the reform was popular.

This reform did little to 'socialize' agriculture. When it was completed, more than three-quarters of all holdings were still privately owned; and of the total of over 2 million private holdings only 29,000 were over 50 acres. The reform had contributed to the fragmentation of landholdings which in itself was a cause of low productivity, since peasant families with very small farms (the majority in scattered strips on the ancient medieval system) had not the capital or equipment to get the most out of their land.[83] The law made provisions to limit subdivision of new holdings by forbidding for a period of twenty years the division, sale, lease or mortgage, partial or entire, of any lands allotted under the new act. But this provision had its bad effect for it prevented the consolidation of strips into homogeneous holdings.

Between 1945 and 1948 the government had no real economic policy for agriculture. This was the period of Soviet-inspired 'bureaucratic centralism', and control of agriculture, like everything else, was attempted from Belgrade and enforced locally by communist officials. Since the Stalinist policy of enforced collectivization had been rejected it was thought to be wiser to leave major decisions on agricultural policy to the future. In the first Five Year Plan, very little investment (8 per cent of the total) was assigned to agricultural production, though it was expected to rise and exceed pre-war levels by 1951. In agricultural methods and choice of crops peasants were left largely to their own devices, which meant that most of them continued to farm with the archaic implements and methods that their ancestors had employed for centuries – hand-sowing, wooden ploughs, little fertilization etc.

Farm machinery and modern implements could not be bought by private peasants. For the most part they were not available since few were made in the country and most imports had to be of raw materials and machinery for the new industries. In any case most peasants could not afford to buy new equipment, and those who could, dare not for fear of being denounced as *kulaks*. Peasants like everyone else at this time were subjected to strict economic controls and a great deal of political propaganda, supervision and pressure.

The most hated regulation at this time was the OTKUP, the system of obligatory sale to the government of a high proportion of each peasant's produce. The peasant received fixed low prices for his food and coupons which enabled him to buy industrial goods, also at fixed low prices. This was the linked prices scheme. The government sold food, also at controlled prices, to townspeople whose rations were limited according to type of work and estimated need. Any surplus left to the peasant after he had fulfilled his OTKUP obligations and his family needs, could be sold on the open market at prices that the government attempted (but entirely failed) to limit. The difference between the prices the peasant got for his food from the government and on the free (and black) markets was immense. Peasants felt the government was robbing them. The system was designed to protect the interests of townspeople in a time of scarcity; to see that food was available for all at prices that compared reasonably with the controlled rates of wages. But this did not interest the peasants who showed no appreciation of the state needs or of their 'duties' to help in establishing socialism. The OTKUP, to make matters worse, was operated with great, perhaps inevitable, inefficiency. The situation developed into a struggle between government officials and peasants. Many farmers were gaoled or fined for black marketing or OTKUP offences.

It was government policy at this time to distinguish between peasants according to the size of their farms. The OTKUP was operated especially harshly against the few peasants who owned larger farms. Peasants were divided into rich, middle or small peasants – the latter being those with less than 10 hectares (24·7 acres), and the rich those with more than 15 hectares (37·1 acres) of land. All peasants were subject to an income tax, and assessment was in the hands of local Communist Party officials who used it as another instrument against 'rich' peasants or any particular political opponent. Even middle and small peasants were not free from pressure; for apart from the OTKUP and income tax they were the main target of government policy to try to persuade peasants to join together and form co-operative or collective farms. The general effect of all these developments was that peasants in general developed an attitude of non-co-operation and passive resistance; they cultivated the minimum possible.

The peasants suspected (and with reason) that the campaign to get them into co-operative farms was designed as a first step in collec-tivization, a means of depriving them of their private property and independence. In fact this was a new communist use for an old idea which had been fairly widespread in the South Slav lands since the nineteenth century. There had been many successful general (buy-ing and selling) co-operative organizations; the first had been founded in Celovec in Slovenia in 1851 – others had been founded in Serbia (1894), in Croatia (1896), Bosnia-Hercegovina (1904), Monte-negro (1907) and Macedonia (1910). Covering all the main South Slav provinces they had had a wide variety of purposes – buying and selling, credit, for special products or processing (viniculture, stock-breeding, agricultural crafts etc.,) and medical and health benefits. Before 1914 there had been 3,500 co-operatives (organized in fifteen unions or groups) in these lands, but they were not for joint owner-ship of land and co-operative farming. They continued to operate during the period between the wars and were regulated by law in 1937. By 1939 Yugoslavia had 11,309 co-operatives, organized into thirty-seven unions with 1,233,637 members, or 63 members for every one hundred peasant families. Co-operatives handled only a small proportion of the sale of produce inside Yugoslavia, but a much higher proportion of export sales. They operated most successfully in Slovenia, Croatia and Vojvodina. All were badly hit by the war; less than half the total number survived (only 5,140) and their assets and activities were greatly restricted.

The idea of co-operatives was therefore a familiar one to all Yugoslav peasants. What was unfamiliar and unacceptable to most peasants was the idea introduced by Tito's government after 1945 that peasants should pool their land. A few of those who received land under the 1945 Reform Act were not unwilling to accept it on condition of forming a co-operative because they had no equipment with which to start on their own and these co-operatives were supplied with all needs by the government.

New communist ideas about co-operatives were defined in a law of June 1946. It provided for four different types of co-operatives – in the first and second of these land joined into a co-operative remained under various conditions the property of its owner, who, as a member of the co-operative, was paid rent or interest on the assessed value of the land he contributed; in the third type no rent was paid to the contributor, who remained the legal owner of his land but only received a share of total profits; in the fourth type the owner transferred his title to the land to the co-operative. In all types, peasants kept their own house and up to one hectare of land depending on the size of the family, but on joining they had to transfer live and dead stock and equipment to the co-operative which paid a purchase price over a period of five years. They were allowed to own one cow with a calf, one sow with a litter, up to fifteen sheep and as many poultry and beehives as they wished.

In the light of what happened later – and worse was to come – regulations about withdrawing from co-operatives were very important. In the first three types members could withdraw after three years subject to three months notice; they must receive their original holding, or land of equivalent value. In the fourth kind members could withdraw after three years but had no right to receive back their own land although given enough land to maintain the family; the value of the original land must be refunded in cash over a period of five to ten years. Very few peasants chose the fourth category when they were persuaded or forced into co-operatives and those who did were mostly those with little to contribute and little to lose by the arrangement.

The idea of communist co-operatives was not taken up with enthusiasm. Numbers rose from 31 in 1945 to 779 in 1947 by which time 210,986 hectares of land had been contributed. Agricultural production in general had risen only very slowly in these years, and both harvests and stock increases were less than expected; they were particularly low on co-operative farms. This was the situation when Yugoslavia was hit by the Cominform quarrel.

In seeking a stick to beat the Yugoslav leaders with, the Soviet communist leadership seized on the question of Tito's policy towards the peasants. Although this had seemed rigorous enough to peasants and outsiders, in the Soviet view it had not been harsh enough.

Yugoslav letters in reply rebutted Soviet criticism indignantly but the leaders were conscious that their policy to the peasants had not been carried to extremes for the simple reasons that they needed the peasants' food and support. This criticism stung Yugoslav leaders into action to prove that they were exemplary communists. Before the heat of the controversy had had time to subside a decision was taken to proceed immediately with the 'socialization' of agriculture; to use every possible method short of legal enforcement to 'persuade' peasants to join co-operatives. A tremendous propaganda campaign was launched in mid-1948 and methods of persuasion were crude and forceful. Numbers of co-operatives rose to 1,318 by the end of 1948; a year later there were 5,246. In 1950 there were 6,075 co-operatives, 404,038 member families with a total of 2,226,166 hectares of land – this represented over a quarter of cultivated land.[84] Serbia (2,022 co-operatives), Croatia (1,395) and Bosnia-Hercegovina (1,265) had the greatest numbers of co-operatives. In

Bosnia-Hercegovina and Croatia many new ones had been founded in the deficit areas where land was poor and farming difficult. Serbian figures were high because they include the Vojvodina where much land had been confiscated from Germans and re-allotted to colonists on condition of co-operative farming. In Slovenia (359) where peasants were thrifty, hardworking and relatively prosperous, co-operatives had little appeal and peasants were strong enough to withstand pressure. The numbers for Montenegro (151) and Macedonia (903) reflected the smaller population and the fact that a much smaller area of land was cultivable. In Macedonia at the peak of the co-operative movement, 60 per cent of both households and land were in co-operatives. Indicative of the pressures used in the formation of co-operatives at this time was the fact that in 1950 the greatest number (3,437, or more than half) were of the third type where neither rent nor interest on value was to be given to members who contributed land. There were still only 358 of the fourth, pure collective type.

Methods of organization and work on the co-operatives were planned by a central organization in Belgrade (Glavni Zadružni Savez) and were the same throughout the country. In theory each farm was run by a General Assembly of heads of households, which elected an executive committee – in larger co-operatives other committees dealt with supervision of labour, finance, building, marketing, forestry etc. In fact the co-operatives were nearly always run by active communists who had been carefully placed in the membership – and had been most active in their foundation.

Work on the co-operative farms was done on a 'brigade' system – with workers, men and women, assigned to a particular group for ploughing, livestock, vegetables, administration etc., for a certain period – a week, a month etc. This led to tremendous friction over comparative effort and responsibility. Payment for work and accounting in general was complicated. Payment was made on a calculation of number of days worked and amount of work that could be expected from an average person. 'Norms' – the expected amount of work – varied from farm to farm and were an endless source of argument and complaint, and questions of who should have what expense accounts were also fruitful sources of indignant dissension. In some co-operatives working days averaged 330 per annum, in others as few as 160 for men; and they varied between 280 and 100 for women who were allowed paid leave for pregnancy and child-birth. In most co-operatives payment was in both cash and kind. A blueprint was issued for allocation of profits at the end of the year; but few co-operatives followed it closely, and few had profits to dispense.

The co-operatives were not a success. By 1951 their numbers were beginning to decline and there was a sinister downward trend in harvests and the amount of land under cultivation. It began to be clear that the whole system of co-operative work on farms of this kind acted as a disincentive to productive hard work. Members were often more interested in working on their own small household plots than co-operatively. Peasants who had formerly walked miles to work on their own strips, refused to go to work on co-operative fields unless transport was provided. The OTKUP was still in force and no more popular with individuals in co-operatives than it had been when they had private farms. At first it was possible to find excuses for the drop in agricultural production – members needed time to get used to the system, the harvest of 1950 was bad due to drought. In 1951 the harvest improved, but after another drought in 1952 harvest figures fell to the lowest peacetime level since 1920, only 40 per cent of the pre-war average and half the level of 1948. One and a quarter million acres had gone out of cultivation, and some of these were on co-operative farms.

There were many reasons for the failure of the co-operative experiment besides the disinclination of peasants to work their hardest under collective conditions. By 1952 the experiment had only been working for about three years in many cases. Financial concessions made by the state were such as to defeat their own ends – loans from the National Bank had been freely available for invest-ment and had been interest free. Working capital was loaned at a nominal 1 per cent interest. By the end of 1951 loans totalled 15,000 million dinars. A great part of this money had been spent on con-structing buildings which did little to increase productivity. In 1951

179

repayment on building loans had to be waived. In any case, loans could not have been spent in this period on machines, stock and fertilizers that would have improved production because foreign currency was not available for their import. Many of those who joined co-operatives for one reason or another – poor land, ignorance and poverty – had had no experience of successful farming. Even successful peasant farmers had rarely had the experience of large scale organizational farming necessary to run a co-operative. The best brains in the country, especially among the communists, had been drafted to work on the industrialization schemes. The co-operatives tended to be run by junior, not very competent or tactful communist officials. Most co-operative members were not Communist Party members; they were individuals, anxious to get a better deal as peasants, they approached the whole experiment with caution, suspicion and half-hearted interest.

By the summer of 1952 many peasants had been in co-operatives for three years and their contract permitted them to withdraw. There was a rush to get out. The first official reaction was one of furious indignation. But by 1952 new political and economic ideas were being tried out and the tide had turned against Stalinism. It was no longer necessary to try to please or outsmart Russia and a realistic approach to economic growth – including a slightly more favourable attitude to agriculture – was already in vogue. By a decree of 30 March 1953 peasants were given the right to withdraw land and livestock from co-operatives. By 1958 only 507 working co-operatives with 501,600 acres of land remained.

'You cannot force peasants, you must convince them', said Tito in a speech to a large peasant audience in Drvar in 1953. It was an admission that earlier policy towards agriculture had been a failure. Peasants had been coerced into co-operatives, but not into greater productivity. This failure and the post-Cominform liberalization produced a new deal for agriculture – more investment, increased incentives, a long-term and more stable policy; but most important of all it produced a changed official attitude towards private peasants, less hostile, more liberal and above all accepting the fact that peasant attitudes can only be changed slowly. It is more than probable that the basic communist theories about land and peasants had not changed; that peasants owning private land were still considered an anomaly in a communist state. But the co-operative experiment had also shown that enforced co-operatives even though they made larger farms did not lead to higher yield. Some other solution had to be found which would produce more food and at the same time not be too much at variance with the 'socialization' that was being applied to the rest of political and economic life. This meant a compromise policy for land and peasant – more free enterprise, and gradual socialization. This, in varying mixtures has been the policy down to the present day.

Liquidation of uneconomic co-operatives and the freeing of un-willing co-operative members was designed to go hand in hand with considerable investment into agriculture – investment that would be available for all kinds of farms, state farms, the few remaining co-operatives and farms belonging to private peasants. In 1953 a ten year plan for agriculture was launched with a 620,000 million dinar investment programme; foreign currency (as well as internal invest-ment) was to be available for import of good quality livestock, tractors, fertilizer, seeds, pesticides etc., until these things could be produced in Yugoslavia in sufficient quantity and of satisfactory quality. The need for good machinery at this time is shown by the fact that in 1953, out of 8,000 tractors in the country (of seventy-three different types), only one third could be used; the rest were either obsolete or in need of repair. Money had also to be found for many other projects – for land reclamation, for irrigation to prevent loss of harvest during drought years, for refrigeration plants and improvements in local communications and transport so that agricultural supplies could be marketed in a rational way.

It was relatively easy for communist leaders to be in agreement on the general lines of investment into agriculture because the country's need for increased food production was almost desperate. The population was increasing by about 140,000 per annum, food consumption of all classes was on the increase, and it was clear by this time that the export of agricultural produce was essential for the country's viability. Industry was certainly expanding, exports increasing, and more industrial items appearing on the home market, but industry was likely for some years to absorb its own profits in further expansion. It was more difficult to get agreement among the leaders on how the general policy should be implemented. Should peasants be encouraged to produce by allowing them to make profits beyond what they needed for subsistence? Some of the leaders (Alexander Ranković, Peter Stambulić, and, surprisingly in the light of later events, Milovan Djilas) were against this and it was some time before unanimous agreement was reached on a new deal for peasants. When it came, it combined money incentives and greater freedom for farmers with a new, more restrictive, Land Law. Although the new law made no attempt to revive Working Co-operatives, it tied all benefits of state subsidies and aid to agriculture to membership of General Co-operatives. This meant that private peasants had to become members of this state organization if they wanted to borrow or buy machinery, receive loans and credits, sell their produce to the state, or take advantage of the many schemes to step up production.

In 1952 there were more than 9,000 General Co-operative Societies in Yugoslavia (Serbia 4,600, Croatia 2,100, Slovenia 1,101, Bosnia-Hercegovina 872, Macedonia 400 and Montenegro 91). Though the total figure showed a drop of about 3,000 since before the war, numbers of societies in the poorer republics, Macedonia and Montenegro, showed a marked increase. Between 1945 and 1953 the General Co-operatives had only a very limited function; they had provided village shops, some had even had shops in towns; but goods for sale in shops had been in short supply and the government had neither used nor aided the General Co-operatives very much, regarding them as a bourgeois institution.

In 1953, General Co-operatives were encouraged to extend their activities and the new political climate of decentralization and economic competition made it possible for them to do so. Government credits at low rates of interest were made available to private peasants through the General Co-operatives; other benefits made available to members were fertilizers (at highly subsidized prices), imported breeding stock to be paid for by their progeny, machinery, and loans for farm buildings and houses. Co/operatives were also encouraged to form new Unions for special activities – co/operatives for pig/farmers, cattle/breeders, viniculture, apiculture, etc., and it was proposed through these to give technical assistance so that quality and quantity of produce could be improved. By the nineteen/ sixties it was claimed that over 95 per cent of all peasant families belong to these General Co/operatives which came to serve a similar political function to that of the Trade Unions in industry.

Whilst government subsidy through the General Co/operatives helped the private peasants to make more money, a new Land Reform Act (May 1953) was passed further restricting the amount of land permitted for private ownership. Any land over 10 hectares (15 in exceptional cases) was expropriated. The object was to get land for the remaining Working Co/operatives which wished to carry on but had been disrupted by private peasants withdrawing their land. 662,611 acres were redistributed under this law; none went to private peasants as in previous redistributions. They were assigned to Working Co/operatives (200,000 acres), to General Co/operatives (109,000 acres), to state farms (242,000 acres), and to other state projects.[85] This law was alarming in its implications for the peasants, who feared it was likely to be repeated until private holdings were completely absorbed. Many reassurances had to be given before this fear was even partially allayed. Other changes were more popular. The OTKUP was abolished in 1951. The system of linked prices went in 1952 and in the following year the govern/ ment fixed minimum prices for agricultural produce instead of price ceilings and the whole machinery for marketing and government purchase was overhauled and improved.

More important was the new system of land taxation. Up to this time taxation of incomes of private peasants had been on the basis of an arbitrary estimate of income (usually made by hostile communist officials) on a graduated scale of 7 per cent of incomes of 30,000 dinars per annum to 75 per cent of income of 800,000 dinars and over. Although there were peasants who made very large profits, they were few. All peasants tried to conceal their earnings but few succeeded. The net result of the system had been to take the profit out of private farming, to leave peasants with no incentive to develop production and no profits with which to expand. In 1952–3 the state collected 18,000 million dinars from 2 million peasant families of whom at least one-third were subsistence farmers. This process had had the disastrous effects on agricultural production already noted. In 1953 a reformed system was to be based on an assessed value of each landholding and its normal productive capacity. If a peasant increased productivity, he reaped the profit and it was therefore in his interest to produce as much as possible. This measure, the most popular among peasants since 1945 gave a real fillip to production. It involved a cadastral survey in all republics, many parts of which had never been properly surveyed before. It still remains the basis of peasant taxation.

At present 90 per cent of farm-land is worked by private peasants, just over 6 per cent by Working Co-operatives, and little more than 3 per cent by state farms. On food production about one-quarter comes from the co-operative and state sectors, three-quarters from private peasants. This means that productivity is higher on the state and co-operative farms than on private holdings which is not surprising since the state sector has advantages in the quality of land, of investment and expert direction. This also enables such farms to withstand more easily the difficulties of drought or bad harvest years.

Present policy is to give to farmers in all sectors assistance with which to increase productivity and to increase the areas under cultivation. Any land available for purchase in the open market is now being brought up by state farms, and by the General Co-operatives which supervise its cultivation (on a co-operative basis) and have powers to lease and manage uneconomic private holdings. For political and economic reasons it is likely that private landholdings in Yugoslavia will continue to be reduced by this slow process. The agricultural revolution which is still in progress is as important in its economic, social and political consequences as the more rapid revolution which has taken place in industry.

8   A Country in Transition

YUGOSLAVIA TODAY is a country in transition. It is impossible to give a picture of life that is true for all of it. Visitors can find conditions varying from the most primitive to ultra-modern, it is unwise to generalize from things seen in one part of the country at one particular time. A general picture has to be fitted together from many different facts and impressions, even then the picture is always changing, for Yugoslavia is a new country, developing rapidly.

Some general ideas can be gained from statistics – but to make statistics live they have to be translated into the lives, homes, and working conditions of the 19 million people that today inhabit a country of 101,547 square miles – roughly the size of the whole area of the British Isles.[86] This is a relatively small population for the size of the country, but it is increasing at the high rate of over 120,000 per annum. The largest of the six republics, Serbia, has the highest population and so on through Croatia, Bosnia-Hercegovina, Slovenia, Macedonia to the smallest in size and population, Montenegro; but within these republics, too many people live in mountain regions which provide a very poor livelihood. The most fertile regions are often the least densely populated. This too is changing, for in the past ten years the town-population in all republics has increased and the population of the country districts decreased. Even so, nearly two-thirds of the population are country dwellers, and over a half live by working on the land.

The structure of the population is very different from that in Great Britain. Yugoslavia has only a small proportion of old people – losses of two world wars have destroyed the generations that would have been old today; nearly three-quarters of the present population is below the age of forty-five, almost equally divided between men and women; there are also more bachelors than spinsters – especially in Serbia, Bosnia-Hercegovina and Macedonia. All republics have more surviving widows than widowers, as can be seen in the many villages where black-clad women still mourn those who were killed in the last war.[87]

In the past, population increase among the South Slavs in peacetime has been limited by a high death rate, especially among infants. In Yugoslavia today, there are on average 22·2 births and 9·9 deaths annually per thousand of population, but the number of infants who die after birth is still high – varying from 140 per thousand in Kosovo-Metohija, 133 in Montenegro, 90 in Macedonia to 29 in Slovenia. It is noticeable too that where the infant death rate is high, the birthrate is also high; these figures are highest in the most under-developed, lowest in the most advanced parts of the country. The areas with the highest infant death rates also have a high rate of illiteracy, especially among women (in people over ten years, 21·9 per cent in Serbia, 32·5 per cent in Bosnia-Hercegovina compared with 12·1 per cent in Croatia and only 1·8 per cent in Slovenia).

Education in health and hygiene, and improved free medical services are helping to lower the death rate and improve the health and physique of all Yugoslavs. Malaria, which killed or debilitated thousands in pre-war days, has been virtually eliminated; even tuberculosis is on the wane. There are more doctors (13,931 in 1961 compared with 6,548 in 1952), many of whom have been trained abroad, but they tend to concentrate in the towns to the detriment of the countryside. Hospitals and clinics of all kinds are more numerous, free vaccination and inoculation services are increasing. Payment for sick benefits in 1962 (including maternity and disability benefits) totalled over 324 million dinars against total insurance payments by workers for sickness benefit of 287·4 million dinars. Above all, the population is eating better than ever before.

The question of standards of living is difficult to determine. Visitors from abroad frequently compare Yugoslav life with what they know at home. Standards thus vary greatly and are often entirely personal. For Yugoslavs the real comparison is with life as it was a few years ago, or in the pre-war period. There is no doubt whatever that for all except the few who formerly belonged to rich or privileged families, standards of living have now greatly improved both in comparison with pre-war standards, and with the nineteen-fifties. The question of how people live is determined by how much money they have to spend, or how much food they get from the land they cultivate, and what this money can buy.

In Yugoslavia today there is a much wider spread between the highest and lowest paid workers than there was up to 1950.[88] It has been recognized that more training, technical skill, and greater responsibility must receive a suitably graded reward. Wages vary from 15,000 dinars a month at the lowest level to well over 100,000 at the highest; but numbers receiving these extreme wages are small—about 1·9 per cent of all workers receive the lowest, only 0·3 the highest. The great majority of workers (over 74 per cent) belong to the middle group earning 25–45,000 dinars a month. Amongst the highest paid are those employed in oil industries, metallurgy and mining, electrical power works, air transport, higher education, and some branches of commerce and export. Lowest wages are earned in agriculture and fishing, in timber, textiles, tobacco industries and in unskilled building work. Highest average wages are earned in Slovenia (which also has most workers earning 100,000 dinars and over per month), lowest are in Macedonia (with large tobacco and timber industries) and Serbia, where earnings are high in the capital, Belgrade, low in the backward areas of Kosovo-Metohija.

Incomes of many self-employed people – writers, craftsmen such as carpenters and plumbers, restaurant keepers and people earning from commerce or tourist trade – are often far in excess of wage-earners' incomes. They are subject to taxation, which increases steeply in the higher income brackets, and avoidance is severely punished. The self-employed, in order to avoid the high contribu-tions required, do not all take advantage of the benefits of the medical and social security system open to state employees. Thus in the final account even high earners are levelled down to a position not greatly above the average.

Income of peasants who cultivate their own land is more difficult to calculate; it varies with the season and the year, according to whether crops and harvests have been good. Average earnings of peasants in 1961 were about 35,000 dinars a month (this includes an estimate of the value of food that peasants will have provided for themselves from their own land); earnings in Slovenia and Croatia are considerably higher than this, and are lower in Bosnia-Herce-govina and Macedonia; but variations above and below the average are great in all parts of the country. The old differences between poor, often starving peasants and relatively prosperous townspeople are disappearing; differences in earning power between intellectual and manual workers have also been narrowed. Since private indi-viduals can no longer own large estates or big industries, and great wealth can no longer be inherited (estates are subject to progressive death duties) the number of wealthy people is confined to those who can earn well. There are a few wealthy and privileged people (only a few of them high state and party officials) but there is little ostenta-tion of wealth in Yugoslavia today. At the other end of the scale it is still possible to see some very poor people. What is most remark-able about Yugoslav society is that it has become, if not egalitarian, at least a society in which social distinctions are small; in which skilled workers, civil servants, professional people and many manual workers, can be considered as one class. Among the rapidly increas-ing townspeople there is no great difference in homes (except perhaps as regards books), little difference between the clothes they wear and the recreations they choose, and into this new society the peasants are being rapidly assimilated.

How does this large class of people spend its income? Heaviest expenditure is on food and clothing. In the nineteen-sixties, quality and quantity of food is good by any standard, and clothing, though not up to western European standards in some respects, is now of a much higher standard than it was a few years ago. Rents are low, most families pay no more than 3–5 per cent of wages for living accommodation. Housing is one of the biggest problems in both town and country and many families have to live in crowded conditions comparable to the worst conditions in large industrial towns in Great Britain. Yugoslavs can still own one house or two flats (and a few still live on the income derived from them), but unused space can be requisitioned, rents are both controlled and taxed, and landlords are obliged to keep rented property in good order.

A feature of modern life which is changing the face of Yugo- slavia in every republic is the immense amount of new (private and public) house building that is taking place. Peasants will no longer tolerate the earth-floored wooden-roofed traditional house of their forbears – most have at least improved their parents' houses, many have turned them into byres and built new houses with money bor- rowed from the government. Electricity is being made available in many of the most remote parts of the country and this immediately changes the way of life of the inhabitants.

Bicycles are everywhere, and motor bicycles are replacing horses; in the towns, with many more families being able to afford motor- cars, traffic, garaging and parking are rapidly becoming problems as they are elsewhere in Europe. Radios are a commonplace in both town and country, and it is possible to meet peasants wearing tradi- tional dress that has not changed for centuries walking along un- paved mountain roads entertaining themselves with transistor sets. There were 23 local broadcasting stations in Yugoslavia in 1962; 2,040,000 radio licences were issued, giving an estimate of 1 set to 9 people; 1,196,000 television licences were sold and television was transmitted from 3 stations. Modern factory-made domestic equip- ment is superseding traditional hand-made utensils everywhere.

All over the country fashions in dress are changing rapidly– with very few exceptions, machine-made cloth has taken the place of the homespun, embroidered cloths of the peasants. In some parts of the country peasants have entirely abandoned their traditional wear except for special festive occasions; elsewhere they have adapted modern clothes to traditional designs – new rubber shoes have taken the place of the leather *opance* worn by peasants for generations; factory-made blouses and permanently pleated skirts have replaced the hand-pleated peasant costume. Many of the elaborate peasants' costumes of earlier years can now only be seen in the museums – for the younger generation in all parts of the country is demonstrating its emancipation by changing over to simpler Western clothes. These changes in dress also help to blur the former differences between town and country people, between those with less, and those with more money.

In this new society, education too is a leveller, for it is free, mixed and the same for children of all income groups (with education for minorities in their own languages). Compulsory school education is based on an eight-year span (7–15) which covers five years primary schooling followed by three years secondary, technical or vocational education. All children who reach a certain standard in primary school may go to grammar school, and, if they complete this course, pass on to university. In 1962 there were 14,568 primary schools with 2,896,000 pupils and 89,611 staff; 275 higher (grammar) schools with 95,000 pupils and 5,512 staff; and 244 universities and colleges – including teachers' training colleges, technical colleges and a number of colleges for specialized training (music, art, agriculture etc) – with 158,010 students and 12,475 staff.[89] There were in addition hundreds of seminars, courses and lectures for adult students organized by the very popular Peoples' and Workers' Universities set up in each of the six republics. If the illiteracy rate amongst the older peasants is still high, the enthusiasm for, and effort being put into education for the younger generations, is immense. On the national level it is seen as the pre-requisite for industrialization and progress to modernization; for the individual it is the key to better jobs and wider horizons than were available to older generations.

Although education is free, parents have to provide books and minor equipment for their children and this is clearly easier for some families than for others. In the country some children have to travel long distances to the nearest school, and sometimes high schools are so far away that pupils have to obtain lodging nearby during the week. Unless they obtain a special grant, this charge also has to be borne by the parents. Grants for students' board and lodging at university, where tuition is free, are also only available in cases of real hardship. Thus, even with free education, many parents have to make sacrifices if they want their children to complete the full course.

The development of education has had an important effect on the position of women in Yugoslavia. The depressed social position of women began to change during the Second World War when they fought alongside men and were used for every kind of duty. After the war, shortage of labour resulted in women being used for many kinds of work – from judges to heavy manual labourers. Communist theory affirms the equality of the sexes, and women were given the vote, made equal with men in all legal matters, and decreed equal pay for equal work. These rights are still strictly enforced in public life, but it does not mean that Yugoslav men have accepted in their private life a principle which to some, especially in the older generation, is abhorrent. Thus Yugoslav women are only slowly coming to play a greater part in public life. A few are found in both federal and republican parliaments; there are increasing numbers in the professions and in the skilled and technical jobs. Twenty-nine per cent of students in higher education are women (compared with about 20·6 per cent in the United Kingdom) and a much higher percentage in teachers' training colleges and the technical schools. But it is still noticeable, as in most other countries of western Europe (and the Soviet Union) that women do not reach the topmost ranks of government. There are only a few women on the federal executive council, and on the executive councils of the six republics. The position of women in the past varied in different regions of the South Slav lands, but it was, and still is, particularly depressed in the Moslem regions of Bosnia-Hercegovina and Macedonia. Legal emancipation of women after 1945 struck at the basis of Moslem male supremacy, and the veiling of Moslem women was forbidden by law in 1951. But habits of male supremacy die hard in Moslem communities, and it is still possible in country districts to see the Moslem husband riding ahead on the donkey whilst his wife walks behind carrying a heavy load. Even in towns it is possible to meet Moslem men who pay lip-service to the new society in public and treat their wives as a chattel in private. Change has come very fast, and education and a new society offer opportunities for many of the young generation of girls to escape the restricted life, in many cases the servitude that was the lot of women in earlier generations.

The dramatic events of the Second World War, and the revolution which has continued ever since have had a stimulating effect on creative talent. War experiences of the Partisans, of civilians, of prisoners in concentration camps, became the subject of deeply moving poetry, of art (drawings, paintings and sculpture), of novels, plays and films. Although many of these were associated with local experiences, the theme was a national one as is shown in the work of Vladimir Nazor (well known before the war), of Kaleb, Mirko Božić, Mihailo Lalić, of Dobricu Ćosić, Miodrag Bulatović and many other writers; and in the field of art in works by Vladimir Veličković, Milic Stanković, to name only two from many.

The two greatest names in post-Second World War literature are Miroslav Krlježa and the Nobel prize-winner Ivo Andrić. Both men were writing before 1941 and both write on themes closely connected with the history or present lives of their own people. Krlježa is a Croat and Andrić a Bosnian but their works have more than a local appeal and both have achieved international fame. Andrić has written many stories and novels about the past history (under Turkish and Austrian occupation) of his native Bosnia – for example, *The Bridge on the River Drina* and *Bosnian Story*. Krlježa's writing – plays, poems, stories and novels – covers a wider field of history and human experience. Among the young writers coming to the fore Oskar Davičo and Marko Ristić may be mentioned.

During the period of Stalinist government (1945–8), and for some years after, the influence of official communist theory was marked on every field of art. The glorification of Marxist society, socialist-realism was required from writers and artists. The fact that the state controlled all publishing and public exhibition of works of art had an inhibiting effect. Authors and artists were given scholarships, salaries were paid for work commissioned by the state, so that they were obliged to produce acceptable works. The system remains the same today, but with the difference that more latitude is allowed for individual creative talent and freedom of expression – short of what is considered subversive or corrupting to society. Interpretation of these later categories varies with changes in the political climate.

Some idea of the present climate of opinion is shown by the fact that since the liberalization of political life, Yugoslav artists (Mica Popović, Ljubo Ivančić, Orden Petlevski and others) have been free to produce abstract works not yet permitted in the Soviet Union or other communist countries in eastern Europe. From time to time this form of art is officially condemned as decadent, but it has in fact become an accepted part of the best post-war art in Yugoslavia. The same trends have been marked in academic work in Yugoslavia – a narrow Marxist approach was required in the early days, and much greater freedom (though still within limits) for individual interpretation has been permitted in the last decade.

Between the two world wars art and literature as well as politics and almost every aspect of life were considered in terms of the different regions of Yugoslavia – of Serbia, Croatia, Slovenia and the other present-day republics. One of the most important questions asked by people who knew Yugoslavia at that time is how far have the regional feuds, hostilities and narrow loyalties of the past been resolved in present-day Yugoslavia? This is another very difficult question to answer. Previous chapters have shown that the political system has been designed to prevent any of the different groups of peoples feeling a grievance; all are equal, all have the same rights of autonomy. The preamble to the 1963 constitution guarantees the right of all peoples to 'self-determination, including the right to secession'.[90] Great care is taken to see that the nationalities are fairly represented in all aspects of state life that are organized on a federal basis. It can no longer be said, as it could of the Kingdom of Yugoslavia, that one nationality has a predominant influence. Complaints can still be heard, for instance, that Montenegrins have a dominating position in Belgrade, but this has no more significance than, say, a complaint in Britain that Scotsmen rule the roost in London. Both Montenegrins and Scots have an incentive to leave their barren native highlands to get on in the world.

Yet old habits die hard – especially in the older generations whose attitudes hardened into antagonisms before the Second World War. There is no doubt that local loyalties are still strong amongst such people, to be found in small numbers in all republics, and they are still quick to see a fancied slight, a favouring of one nationality against another. Great vigilance is still required to see that people of influence do not favour their own countrymen unduly, or provide fuel for complaints.

Many aspects of the new society are working to break down such exclusive regionalism. School education includes a study of history of the particular region where the schools are, but it also encourages the study of Yugoslav history, and children are taken on school journeys so that they know what other parts of the country are like; higher education – universities and technical colleges – television and radio programmes and newspapers all help to create a concept of nationality which does not exclude regional loyalties. The fluidity of labour in present-day Yugoslavia means that people travel more as they change their jobs. Mixed marriages between people of different regions are becoming increasingly common. The 1953 Census gave figures of people describing their nationality as follows: 6,983,544 Serbs, 3,913,733 Croats, 1,462,961 Slovenes, 2,843,486 Bosnians, 1,303,906 Macedonians and 419,625 Montenegrins; but it cannot be assumed that these people were all living and working in their own regions.[91] These divisions were not given in the census of 1963. It seems to be inevitable that as the country is increasingly modernized the mixture of people will weaken the purity of exclusive regional nationality that remained as long as each region lived, as in the past, its own inbred local life.

The mixture of population resulting from modern industrial society has only taken place over two or three generations and no great change can yet be expected in conditions that have persisted for hundreds of years. It is probable that the country could still become bitterly divided and again disintegrate into its regional and confessional groupings, if there were to be international or civil war. This is one of the reasons why Tito's government does not allow free development for political parties; it is believed, and probably with reason, that they would help to perpetuate old, and breed new regional rivalries. Even with the one-party system, and strictly enforced laws against racial hatred, the present society does offer many opportunities for regional rivalry, and perpetual vigilance is required to see that it does not get out of hand.

The most fruitful field for local rivalry and grievance is in the division of federal funds for economic development. Some parts of the country – Montenegro, Macedonia and Bosnia-Hercegovina have been much more underdeveloped than Slovenia, Serbia and Croatia. They have been assigned a correspondingly larger proportion of federal funds for industrial projects. Some people in the more pros-perous republics whose enterprises pay more taxation because of their higher profits, have resented this. The 1963 earthquake in Skopje, for example, did 10,000 million dinars worth of damage,[92] which could clearly not be paid from local funds, and became an extra charge (10 per cent of investment over five years) on the federal budget. This involved sacrifices from other republics which meant cutting their own plans for development; it also brought many problems for the local authorities of Skopje (capital of the Macedonian republic) who wanted immediate federal money to build an ambitiously designed new city. This was a classical example of the apparent conflict of interest between the federal government which had to enforce sacrifice on other republics and the Macedonian government, which believed that its people deserved every possible sacrifice and consideration from the rest of the country. The compromise and consideration required to solve such problems without creating too much regional resentment is typical of the present-day Yugoslav scene. But it constitutes a problem which is also faced in other countries (e.g. southern and northern Italy). The major difference in Yugoslavia is in the very recent background of lack of unity, the short period that the Yugoslav nation has existed.

The Communist Party and the larger organization, the eight million strong Socialist Alliance of the Working People, through which it approaches the general body of people, are a very important influence in developing the growth of national unity. The real test of nationalism comes in times of crisis; it is notable that during the two major foreign affairs crises that Yugoslavia has experienced since 1945 (Trieste and the Cominform dispute), the Yugoslav people reacted with remarkable national unanimity. A more searching test will come when a successor has to be found for President Tito, whose personal influence towards national unity has been immense.

In the past, religion amongst the South Slavs was often a cause and instrument of regional rivalry. This was still a feature of life under the royalist régime between 1918 and 1945. During these years Catholics (of Croatia and Slovenia) considered that the Orthodox Church was unduly favoured because it was the religion of the Serbs and of the ruling family. After 1941, during the Second World War the terrible lengths to which religious hatred could be carried were seen in the forcible conversions carried out by Catholic Ustaše in the so-called Independent State of Croatia where many Orthodox Christians were slaughtered for refusing to become Catholics.

In the pre-war Kingdom also, both Orthodox and Catholic Churches were rich, privileged and influential. Both had large holdings in real estate, owned banks, printing presses, schools, colleges, and had considerable industrial holdings. The Serbian Orthodox Church received generous subsidies from the state and the proceeds of a tax on members similar to the church tithe. The Catholic Church in Yugoslavia also received much money from its adherents as well as a general subsidy (from Rome) as a missionary domain (*terra missionis*). Mutual hatred and rivalry between the two churches was very strong.

It is against this background that religious developments in Yugoslavia since 1945 have to be considered. Such aspects of the temporal activities of the churches made it easier for the Communist Party to justify its anti-religious doctrine. But for the general body of Yugoslav people, religious faith has very deep roots, and though church going has declined greatly since pre-war days, it is fairly certain that most Yugoslav people, except the communists and few agnostics, still consider themselves as belonging to a religious faith.

In the 1953 census, figures for the different faiths were as follows: Orthodox 41·5 per cent (about 7 million), Catholic 31·8 per cent (5·4 million), Moslem 12·3 per cent (2·1 million), Protestant 0·9 per cent (150,000), other faiths 1·2 per cent (200,000); and 12·3 per cent (2·1 million) described themselves as without religion. Comparable figures for 1963 are not obtainable.

Since 1945 the struggle has been between church and state, with the communist controlled state exerting heavy pressure to dislodge the churches from their previous position of political and social influence, to force them into a position no Christian (or Moslem) church had ever before held in the South Slav lands: this was that their field of operation was to be purely in matters of faith and religious observance. Since Christian missionaries first came to work among the South Slavs, the churches, Orthodox and Catholic, had been great land-owners. Under the Turkish régime, the Moslems had also had extensive church-owned lands – the *vakuf*. These religious land-holdings were drastically cut down in successive land reform acts (1945 and 1953); church property became subject to the same limitations as those of individual holders. Other church property – and this was considerable – was nationalized in 1945.

Many other political, social and economic measures of the communists were anathema to the various organized religions. State marriage, secular education, equality of the sexes (for Moslems especially), insistence of the secularization of public life (the great feast days of the church were not accepted as public holidays), on material development – all these ran counter to the traditions of centuries, and the churches, especially the Catholic Church, were not prepared to give up their privileged position without a struggle. Moreover, for the Catholic Church, but not for the Orthodox, communism itself became a proscribed political organization which meant that, in theory at least, Yugoslavs could not be both Communists and members of the Catholic Church. Many in fact have tried to be both as is shown by frequent denunciations by the Communist Party of party members who have their children baptized, their relatives buried, or are themselves married by the Churches.

The battle between the Catholic Church and the state was joined immediately after the liberation in 1945. On 20 September the Yugoslav Catholic Bishops led by Mgr Stepinac, Archbishop of Zagreb, issued a Pastoral Letter attacking the Partisans and their policies. On 24 September Stepinac was arrested on charges of having collaborated with the Pavelić régime in Croatia during the war, and of having blessed the Ustaše troops who had forcibly converted the civilian population and committed notorious atrocities.

At the trial, many people testified that Stepinac (whose association with the Pavelić régime was not denied) had also helped Jews and other refugees to escape their persecutors during the war. On 11 October 1946 Stepinac was found guilty and sentenced to sixteen years imprisonment; he was released in December 1951 on condition that he returned to his native village of Krašić (not to his See of Zagreb) which he was not allowed to leave. He was able to minister as priest but free access to the village was not allowed.[93]

In the intervening years (1945–51) during the period of Stalinist communism the Catholic Church experienced the full rigours of anti-religious policy. Many priests were persecuted for doing what they considered to be their duty; local communists often exceeded official instructions in suppressing what they considered to be anti-state activities of the church. The Catholic Church and state stood for opposing beliefs; many priests felt in conscience bound to preach against the new state and use their great spiritual influence to undermine state authority over their flock. On 17 December 1952 the government broke off diplomatic relations with the Holy See on the grounds that it was encouraging subversive activity in its churches in Yugoslavia. Relations were still not restored in 1964.

After 1952, following the liberalization of Yugoslav communism, relations with the Catholic Church improved slowly; very gradually both church and state came to adopt less intransigent positions, so that by the nineteen-sixties a guarded *modus vivendi* had become possible. Bishops and priests were allowed greater freedom in carrying out their religious duties, organizing their churches and administering their limited property and revenues. The Roman Catholic Church in Yugoslavia today has 4 archbishoprics, 15 bishoprics, 4 apostolic administrations, 13 provincialships and inspectorates of male-orders, about 2,500 parishes, 7,702 churches and chapels, and 375 monasteries; there are 5,870 nuns (many of them in great demand as nursing sisters in hospitals run by their orders) and only 685 friars or monks, the greater part of them old men. The Catholic Church also has 2,155 students training to be priests in 33 religious training schools.[94]

The Catholic Church has refused to allow its priests to join the state insurance system; it maintains itself on income accruing from land and property and by contributions from its followers and from supporters abroad. It does, however, accept money from the state for the upkeep of its churches and monasteries which are considered as part of the nation's historical heritage. Relations with state authorities have greatly improved. Religious education, though not allowed in schools, can be organized by priests. Churches in the Catholic parts of Yugoslavia on Sundays and Christian feast days are very full but the number of young people in attendance has decreased.

Throughout history, the Orthodox Church has been more willing than the Catholics to accept the authority of the state and the struggle between the Yugoslav state and the Orthodox Church has therefore been much less intractable. The Serbian Orthodox Church is autonomous, with its own synod consisting of representatives of the twenty eparchies and monasteries and its own elected Patriarch. Most members of this church are in Serbia and Montenegro but it also has members (and Bishops) in Bosnia-Hercegovina, and in Croatia. The Serbian Orthodox Church has 21 bishops, 1,850 priests, 2,974 churches and chapels, 144 monasteries with 293 monks and 552 nuns – these figures do not include statistics for Macedonia which has its own independent organization, and has 3 bishops, 221 priests, 745 churches, 70 monasteries and only 80 monks and nuns. It also has 3 schools for training candidates for the priesthood.[95]

State regulations about religion, the limitation of land-holding, and nationalization of industries affected the Orthodox Church in the same way that they did the Catholic. Churches became very much poorer and the numbers of monks and nuns and candidates for priesthood declined. In the years immediately after 1945 the Orthodox Church was also persecuted and oppressed; but it was the first church to make an agreement with the government. As a result Orthodox priests and their families (for many are married) participate in the state social insurance system and are entitled to the health services, sickness benefits and pensions. The Orthodox Church also receives financial aid from the state (83 million dinars in 1960 compared with 78 million dinars to the Catholic Church).[96] Much of this is used for the preservation of ancient buildings.

A similar sum (over 76 million dinars in 1960) was also received by the Islamic community in Yugoslavia. Like the Christian religions, the Moslems have had difficulty in accepting many of the policies of the authoritarian, secular communist state. The Moslem community in Yugoslavia is autonomous; up to 1945 it was composed of many different religious and educational bodies. As secular and educational power was taken from the community the need for reformed organizations became pressing and a new constitution integrating all Moslem bodies into a simplified organization was passed by the Supreme Council (consisting of thirty-five representatives of local bodies) of the Islamic community on 13 July 1959. The Islamic religion in Yugoslavia today has 2,000 religious officials, and 2,077 mosques; it elects its own chairman, the Reis-ul-Ulema, whose residence is at Sarajevo in Bosnia, and who represents the whole Islamic community in dealings with the state. Mosques in Yugoslavia are regularly attended, and every day the muezzin is to be heard calling the faithful to prayer from minarets in all Moslem parts of the country.

If it is possible to generalize about the position of religion and the churches in Yugoslavia today it may be said that religious observance may be practised freely, as crowded churches and mosques show. The churches have however lost their secular power, riches and prestige – a position which they continue to lament and probably resent. The effect of communist education almost certainly means that an increasing number of young people grow up as non-believers and the weakened position of the churches is shown in the declining numbers of young candidates for the novitiate in religious communities and for religious orders. The state does not persecute the churches; it gives them the means of subsistence; but at the same time it does nothing to encourage, and in the field of propaganda much to discourage, the spread of religious belief. The churches in varying degrees have accepted this (for them) unsatisfactory *modus vivendi*, but it is probably true that all would be in some measure openly hostile to the communist state if they were given the opportunity to be so.

81 Peasants owning private
land participated in co-
operative or collective
farming. A tobacco farm
at Kumanovo in Mace-
donia.

82 The harvest on the
mountain slopes of Bosnia-
Hercegovina illustrates
some of the difficulties of
cultivation.

83 Primitive methods of cultivation are still used.

84 This is gradually being replaced with modern equipment. The large agricultural-industrial land holding at Belje in Croatia.

85 Peasants working with the organizers of a co-operative farm.

86 Modern methods of breeding pigs at Belje.

87 This new school at Zagreb is one of the many schools which provide free education (*left*).

88 The kindergarten at the mining town of Raša (*left below*).

89 Four days after an attack on the Partisan movement in September 1945, Mgr Aloysius Stepinac, Archbishop of Zagreb, was arrested on charges of having collaborated with the Nazis during the war. He was subsequently tried, found guilty and sentenced to sixteen years imprisonment (*right*).

90 Both the Catholic and Orthodox Churches are tolerated by the state but the latter has always been more inclined to accept state authority. A group of clergy leave St Mark's Church, Belgrade, after a service during the rebuilding of the city (*below*).

91 Milovan Djilas one of Tito's strong supporters during the war and subsequently Vice-President leaves the courtroom with his sister (left) and wife in 1955 having been sentenced to three years suspended imprisonment for criticizing the government.

92 Friendly relations began to develop between the Soviet Union and Yugoslavia after the death of Stalin. Mr Krushchev makes a speech on a visit to Belgrade in 1955 in which he expresses regret for the rift which had existed between the two countries.

93 Official talks at the Kremlin in 1956.

94 Yugoslavia takes a leading rôle amongst the non-aligned nations of the world. President Tito (far right) with (left to right) Mr Nehru, President Nkrumah, President Nasser, President Sukarno at a meeting in New York in 1960.

9   Communism and Communists

THE PRESENT-DAY YUGOSLAV political system is officially
described as 'socialist democracy'. These words have a different
connotation from the meaning usually given to them in Western
usage. In Yugoslavia today 'socialism' means a stage in communist
development before full communism has been reached; democracy
means that the people participate in government – by elections,
representatives in government at all levels etc. – but it does not imply
full freedom of political choice or freedom to change the basis of
political power.

Since 1945 political power in Yugoslavia has been in the hands
of the Communist Party and everyone has to accept its basic ideas
of government. No other political organization is allowed. In the
early years (1948–50) when internal and external conditions required
strong government, the communists themselves exercised all power.
Since 1952, government has been more broadly based and many
non-communists have been brought to play a part in the executive
functions of government. Government has been decentralized and
an attempt is being made to base it on acceptance and consent.
Although ultimate political power is still in the hands of the communists, great attempts have been made to make the system of
government more popular – more liberal and far less restrictive
than before; there has been much more fluidity, experiment and
change in methods of administration. The political system is still in
evolution and it may be assumed that one of the aims is to create a
system still under communist control but sufficiently acceptable to

sufficient numbers of people to ensure its continuity when Tito dies.

Although Tito has never been the theoretician of the revolution – this has been left to Edward Kardelj and others – he has always been the architect, inspiration and undisputed leader. He has been interested in the end product – a modern state with decent economic conditions and equality of opportunity for all citizens; and he has been prepared to use many different methods and a certain amount of compromise to achieve this. In the process, a national form of communism has been evolved – which some would deny is communism. There is no doubt that Tito has come to be considered both internationally and nationally as much a leader of the Yugoslav nation as of the Yugoslav communists.

It is a remarkable fact that the majority of communist leaders that Tito collected round him before and during the war are still working with him today. Some, like Moša Pijade and Boris Kidrić, have died. A number of leading communists have at one time or another been in disagreement with certain policies, but the principle that a majority decision must be loyally accepted by the minority has been enforced and no communist has been allowed to carry opposition into action. How far Tito's own personality has had the effect of maintaining agreement is impossible to say, but it has probably played a great part.

There have been defections. Two communist critics of the first Five Year Plan, Sreten Žujović and Andrija Hebrang, were imprisoned in 1948 when their views brought them into line with Soviet criticisms of the Yugoslav Party. An army general and former Chief of Staff, Arso Jovanović, also supported the Soviet position and he was shot whilst trying to flee the country. Other less important communists also fled at that time and many were imprisoned. It is probable that there is always present in the Yugoslav Communist Party a small group of extreme purists who do not agree with the liberal interpretation of Titoist communism, but their existence can only be guessed, for the system does not allow open expression of radical disagreement.

The only member of the innermost circle of Tito's leadership who has broken with the communists has been Milovan Djilas, and his difference with the party has been for quite different reasons. Djilas is in prison (1964) because he came to disapprove of many aspects of communist society. This led him to reject the communist monopoly of power and he wanted to work for a democratization (in the Western sense) of the Yugoslav system of government. Djilas's ideas appealed to many people and he had a forceful and attractive personality. His colleagues feared that he might get a following, that such ideas could easily lead to the return of political disunity, the instability of pre-war days and the loss of all the achievements of the revolution. His ideas threatened the whole existing system and power of the Communist Party.

Milovan Djilas (born 1911) is a Montenegrin who worked with Tito before and during the war; in the post-war period he was Vice-President, Minister without portfolio, one of the most important communist leaders, enjoying a unique freedom to express his views. In the Cominform dispute, he supported Tito and was one of the Yugoslav leaders most denounced by the Russians. His position of critic within the Party was at first accepted and his early attacks on features and injustices of communist government were published in official publications. He criticized the growth of a new privileged class under communism, declaring that party officials and their families formed a milieu where 'character and personal worth are rated by the rank a person holds in the hierarchy, and above all by the actual power a person wields'.[97]

When Djilas moved from general criticisms to personal attacks on party officials and their wives, he was considered to have gone too far. He was sentenced to three years' suspended imprisonment (January 1955) and later resigned from the party. During these years his views developed further away from his former colleagues and he came in the end to the view that the abuses were inherent in the communist system, based as it was on a monopoly of power. He was imprisoned in 1957 for publishing abroad views hostile to the state, and though he was conditionally released in 1961 he continued to publish. He was imprisoned again in the following year. There were many occasions when Djilas could have left Yugoslavia had he wished; he could have led a restricted but free life as a private citizen but he deliberately chose the martyrdom of imprisonment as a protest of passionate disillusionment because the Yugoslav communist state had not realized his idealistic hopes. Djilas's case shows the limits to political freedom in the Yugoslav state. His treatment would certainly have been harsher in other communist states.

The power of the communists is exercised through the League of Communists (as the Communist Party is now called) which has a membership of 1,018,331 and a controlling influence in all other important social and political organizations such as the Socialist Alliance of the Working People (7,025,566 members, formal membership of which shows general acceptance of communist principles), the Trade Unions, Youth Federation (1,636,544 members from whom new communist members are recruited), women's and professional organizations.[98] It also has an important controlling position in the armed services and militia, and in the security services.

The League of Communists is officially described as 'the leading political organization of the working class and working people of Yugoslavia'; its aim is to 'fight for the development of socialist society and for its evolution towards communism.'[99] It is organized into 'leagues' or parties – federal, republican, district and local (municipal, commune or smaller units of not less than three people); it also has 'basic organizations' in all factories or works, in every kind of public service including the civil service, schools and all educational institutions. The organization provides for communists to keep an eye on social and recreational groups so that it can influence people in every aspect of organized public life. Where it is not possible to form a party, communists may be designated as 'actives' to influence thought and activities of any particular group – for example school boards, committees of tenants, groups of jurists, economists etc.[100]

In the early phases of the revolution, up to 1948 and well into the nineteen-fifties, such communist organization and activities were kept secret. Communists were regarded as hostile spies and informers. They probably regarded themselves as a political *élite* and they accepted as no less than their due the privileges and material advantages (better housing, even communist shops with better goods, cars, larger salaries etc.) which went with their position.

Since their Sixth Party Congress in 1952 the Communist Party leaders have made great efforts to change this attitude, and the far from favourable image it created in the public mind. Facts about Communist Party membership, meetings and organization are now made public. Although this information about communist activities is clearly not total, and is selected to project a new image it presents a very different situation from the earlier days. This congress was particularly important for it marked the change between the old communist outlook and the new. Communists were instructed that they were not an *élite*, and were not to behave as if they were. The party changed its name to League of Communists and was told that it was 'less a factor of authority and more a factor in the forma, tion and development of the socialist awareness of the working people'. Since then one of the major problems of leadership has been to get communists to accept this new image of themselves and at the same time to prevent them from backsliding into laxness. Many instructions (some published in official papers) have been issued to party members to correct what are described as 'incorrect attitudes'; and one of the important tasks of the party is to keep a watch on the behaviour of its own members.

With the passage of time the ex-Partisans whose communist fer, vour was based on war-time experiences and comradeship became less important than the many new young people who have entered the party in recent years; for them the war is only a part of national history. It is more difficult to give these people the crusading spirit necessary to work for the general good without receiving material rewards. This explains the vigilance maintained within the party and the continual efforts that are made to keep communists interested, active and informed by means of lectures, debates, weekend schools and classes of all kinds.

Thus the power and influence of the communists are not left to chance. They are fostered and extended by perpetual vigilance and a continuous process of watchful selection, organization, indoctrina, tion, covering all citizens in all of their public activities. New members are recruited from young people, and from the increasing numbers of non-communists who are elected representatives on any of the many committees – communal, district, republican, Workers' Councils etc. Today, roughly a third of members of such public bodies are members of the League of Communists.[101]

Of the total party membership of over one million in 1960, 16·7 per cent were women, nearly 50 per cent were members who worked in enterprises (mostly industry) or were members of communes, 11·6 per cent were people who lived in the country (some peasants, but mostly employed or in administrative positions) and over 19 per cent were men and women in educational institutions. About 32 per cent of the entire membership was described as office workers. Of the new members recently admitted to the League over 63 per cent were under the age of twenty-five, and over 85 per cent below thirty years of age. There are no recent figures for people dropped from the party, but it may be assumed that there is some wastage of membership for demands on members' time, energies and interests are very high, and the sacrifices of private life and interests entailed when an individual joins the party are considerable.

The League of Communists (LYC) has its own constitution and system of government; though it is entirely separate from government institutions there can be few important officials in the League who do not also hold important positions in public life. Local parties have to hold an annual plenary conference for election of officers (secretary and deputy) and a secretariat of from five to nine members; elections are by secret ballot, open if proposed by one-third of members and voted by the meeting. Party meetings are usually held monthly.[102]

The supreme body of the LYC is the congress required to be held every five years, and between congresses the supreme authority is the Central Committee (135 members) which has a secretary general (Tito) and two secretaries (Edward Kardelj and Alexander Ranković); it also elects its own executive committee (15 members among whom are representatives of all six republics), and a secretariat, of the executive committee consisting of Tito, Kardelj, Ranković Ivan Gosnjak and Svetozar Vukmanović-Tempo.

The constitution states that the decisions 'of the Congress and the Central Committee of the League of Communists of Yugoslavia are binding upon the Leagues of Communists (local parties) of the peoples' republics'.[103] The LYC is organized 'according to the principles of democratic centralism'; a further statute makes this more explicit: 'the minority is obliged to accept and enforce the decisions of the majority; the organizations and lower bodies are under the obligation to enforce the decision of the higher bodies'.[104]

Since the YCP congress meets only every five years (not always then) effective authority is exercised by the Central Committee, its executive committee and in the final issue by its five-man secretariat whose decisions are accepted by all the lower bodies in the descending hierarchy. This is the hard-core of communist power in Yugoslavia today; it is backed by an efficient army, police and militia. In the past Yugoslavia could be described as a police state. This would not be true today (1964) although there are still many restrictions on individual liberty. It could rapidly be transformed into a police state if danger threatened the present régime. For the present the régime makes efforts to achieve popularity and to give the general people, communists and non-communists alike, a better life, thereby hoping to secure at least acceptance and tolerance for a system of government which it is claimed has brought great benefits to the country.

The Yugoslav system of government is designed to keep power in the hands of the communists whilst at the same time allowing the participation of a high proportion of the people in its administration. The delicate balance between communist leadership and mass participation requires great skill in direction. Up to the present this has been amply supplied by the man who has led the Yugoslav communist revolution for over a quarter of a century – Josip Brož-Tito.

Tito's career has shown him to be one of those political leaders who can be described as great. This is a comment both on his achievements and on his very complex character. He has combined ruthless determination to follow a single-minded aim with a humanity and in some respects liberal outlook unusual in communist leaders. Although he has eliminated enemies who could have prevented him achieving his aim, he has never showed a lust for power for its own sake. There have been no blood baths in Yugoslavia; excesses at the end of the war in paying off old scores were inherent in the situation and compared with other revolutions, not extensive. Tito had then and still has a remarkable authority over his followers; the discipline, even puritanical asceticism, remarked by foreign observers among the Partisans during the war stemmed from Tito's authority which has often since been used to curb extremists amongst his own communists.

As head of state Tito enjoys the trappings of such a position – the houses, cars and every material benefit. He admits to a love of good clothes and probably believes in maintaining the prestige of his position by some display, but there is no evidence that he has become addicted to luxury or materially corrupted by power. No public parade or propaganda is allowed to be made about his present private life with his third wife, and this follows the pattern of his whole life in which family affairs have always been kept strictly apart from his political career. Tito has two children and many relations but none have appeared in eminent positions in the state.

The reasons why Tito became a communist can be found in what we know about his childhood when he saw and experienced the social injustice and frightful economic conditions of the poor in the Austro-Hungarian Empire at the beginning of this century. Tito was born in 1892, the seventh of fifteen children of peasants living in the Croatian village of Kumrovec in Zagorje on the borders of Croatia and Slovenia, both at that time under Austro-Hungarian rule.[105] His father was a Croat, his mother a Slovene. This mixed parentage, and the fact that he travelled much in later life have meant that he has never had a narrow regional loyalty like so many other South Slav people. Tito was brought up and educated (from the age of 7 to 12 in a village school with 350 children to one teacher) as a Catholic; he was apprenticed as a locksmith and worked as a mechanic before the First World War in Croatia, Austria, and Germany. German was as much a native language to him as Croatian. He did his military service in the Austro-Hungarian army in 1913 and during the war became a non-commissioned officer and fought on the

Russian front where he was wounded and taken prisoner. Later in life as an underground communist leader in the nineteen-thirties he travelled extensively in western Europe. He thus has a deep personal knowledge of Western culture and its people. This is rare in communist leaders. Rare also is the fact that he lived for long periods in Russia, both during the Russian revolution and in the terrible Stalinist years of the nineteen-thirties. He became fluent in Russian and learnt about life under Soviet rule from the inside. The combination of these two extremes of experience is almost unique in a communist leader (the Bulgarian Dimitrov being the only one who had similar experience) and it enabled him when he became head of the Yugoslav State to understand both Western and Eastern developments.

Dislike of many aspects of Western capitalism and Soviet communism led to the evolution of the particular brand of Yugoslav communism that is today known as Titoism. Only a man of great courage could have dared attempt such an experiment, only great ability and loyal support from a comparatively large personal following could have brought it to its present degree of success.

Tito has also had a large element of luck in his life. He was lucky not to be killed when pierced by a Cossack's lance in the First World War, lucky to have escaped death in many forms in the Second World War; lucky to have escaped being executed as a dangerous underground communist leader between the two wars; lucky to have escaped Stalin's purge in the thirties; lucky not to have been assassinated by one of the many enemies of Yugoslav communism and lucky to have had the health to survive to be an old man.

It is impossible to say if Tito is personally popular in Yugoslavia. His close associates refer to him with affection and call him 'stari', the old man. In his present eminent position he is inevitably far removed from ordinary people and he has in any case for the greater part of his life accepted responsibilities that have made him a man apart. South Slav people have never given much personal adulation to their leaders; but they have often made myths of them, and Tito has become a myth in his own lifetime – a myth that has a certain

Notes on the text

I CROSS-ROADS OF EAST AND WEST

1 Balkan in Turkish means 'mountain'

2 One of the main sources is the chronicle of the Eastern Emperor Constantine Porphyrogenitus (948): *De Administrando Imperio*, edited by G. Moravcsik, Budapest, 1949 (translated by R. J. H. Jenkins, 1949)

2 THE REPUBLICS AND THEIR PAST

3 One of the most comprehensive of the many books of reproductions of Yugoslav church frescoes is *Yugoslavija Srednovakovne Freske*, edited by D. Talbot Rice and S. Radojčić, New York Graphic Society for UNESCO, Paris, 1955. See also D. Talbot Rice's *Art of the Byzantine Era*, London, 1963

4 'The Code of Stephen Dušan', translated into English and edited by Malcolm Burr in *The Slavonic and East European Review*, 1950, vol XXVIII, No 70, pp 198–217, and No 71, pp 516–39

5 The Catholic Franciscan monastery at Fojnica in Bosnia has an interesting collection of trophies of the Turkish period. Restrictions applied equally to all Christian churches, Catholic or Orthodox

6 1 yoke = 0·5755 hectare

7 This has been established by recent researches into the rich collection of Dubrovnik documents; Irmgard Manken, *Dubrovački Patriaziat u XIV veku*, published by Srpska Akademija Nauka, Belgrade, 1960

8 Strabo 7, quoted in J. Gardner Wilkinson, *Dalmatia and Montenegro*, 2 vols, London, 1848, vol I, p 41

9 Rebecca West, *Black Lambs and Grey Falcon*, 2 vols, London, 1942, vol I, pp 115–270

10 See ed. D. Warriner, *Contrasts in a Changing Society*, London, 1964, section on Yugoslavia by P. Auty

11 The major work in English on this subject is D. Obolensky, *The Bogomils:*

A study in Balkan Neo-Manichaeism, Cambridge, 1948. It deals mainly with Bogomilism in Bulgaria. Problems of its development in Bosnia (in Serbia Bogomilism was less developed and of shorter duration) are dealt with briefly in Appendix IV. See also D. Talbot Rice, *The Bogomils*, London, 1962

12 See G.M. Mackenzie and A.P. Irby, *Travels in the Slavonic Provinces of Turkey in Europe*, London, 1877, and A.J. Evans, *Through Bosnia and the Hercegovina on Foot*, London, 1876

13 About 75 per cent of all Moslems were free peasants, but many lived (like the Christians) in conditions of great poverty. See P. F. Sugar, *Industrialization of Bosnia-Hercegovina 1875–1878*, Seattle, 1963, pp 3–6

14 See P. Sugar, op. cit., pp 101–90

15 A.A. Paton, *Highlands and Islands of the Adriatic*, 2 vols, London, 1849, vol I, p 70

16 P. Njegoš, *The Mountain Wreath*, translated into English by J.W. Willis, London, 1930

17 The *bratsvo* was any grouping by kinship or blood brotherhood

18 M. Djilas, *Land without Justice*, London, 1958, p 25. The part played by Milovan Djilas in present-day Yugoslavia is considered below. See also M.E. Durham, *Some Tribal Origins, Laws and Customs of the Balkans*, London, 1928, pp 153–84, and *passim*

19 See M. Djilas, op. cit., pp 59–67

20 An account of the political problems of Macedonia is given in E. Barker, *Macedonia; its place in Balkan Power Politics*, London, 1950

3 THE KINGDOM OF YUGOSLAVIA

21 F. Šišic, *Dokumenti, Matica Hrvatske*, Zagreb, 1920, pp 1–3 and 5–6

22 Ivo Lederer, *Yugoslavia at the Paris Peace Conference; A Study in Frontier-making*, New Haven, 1963, gives details of the negotiations after the First World War

23 This is the official figure of the 1921 census. Yugoslavia was then a little smaller than it is today

24 Figures of 1921 census, quoted in J. Tomasevich, *Peasants, Politics and Economic Change in Yugoslavia*, Stanford and Oxford, 1955, p 285

25 In 1923 Radić joined his party to the Soviet-inspired Peasant International. The Croat Peasant Party kept the word 'Republican' in its title until 1925, after which it was known as the Hrvatska Seljačka Stranka (HSS)

26 The other two regents were Radenco Stanković and Ivan Perović

27 Figures quoted by J. Tomasevich, op. cit., p 242

28 See D. Warriner, 'Urban Thinkers and Peasant Policy in Yugoslavia 1918–1959', *The Slavonic and East European Review*, vol XXXVIII, No 90, December 1959. See also J. Tomasevich, op. cit., pp 367–9

29 J. Tomasevich, op. cit., p 295

30 G. Ciano, *Ciano's Diary 1939–1943*, London, 1947, pp 41–117
    V. Maček, *In the Struggle for Freedom*, New York, pp 187–90

31 Hansard, 3 May 1941

32 *Pregled Istorije Saveza Komunista Jugoslavije*, Institut za Izučavanje Radničkog Pokreta, Belgrade, 1963, pp 46–69

33 The Minister of the Interior, Milorad Drašković, was assassinated by a communist (who, according to Party sources, was acting privately, not under Party orders) in July 1921

34 60,000 is the official figure. In a report to the Third International, Moscow, 22 June–12 July, Sima Marković, representing the YCP, had claimed that it had had a membership of 80,000

35 V. Dedijer, *Tito Speaks*, London, 1953, p 104

36 See *Pregled Istorije SKT*, op. cit., pp 271–8

37 A full history of the Yugoslav Communist Party has not yet been published in any language. Material for this chapter has been taken mainly from the following sources:
    Pregled Istorija SKJ, op. cit.
    J. Marjanovic Potsednik: *Iz istorije Kommunistiĉke Partije Jugoslavije (1919–41)*, Rad, Belgrade, 1953
    J.B. Tito, *Political Report of the Central Committee of the Communist Party of Yugoslavia*, Belgrade, 1948, pp 1–49
    V. Dedijer, op. cit., pp 1–79
    Istorijski Arkiv Kommunistiĉke Partije Jugoslavije, vols 1–24, published in Belgrade between 1949 and the present day
    Regional Communist Party groups in Yugoslavia are also publishing their local archives

38 He fled abroad in 1945, settled as an exile in USA, and died in 1964

39 J.B. Tito, op. cit., pp 50–4

40 V. Dedijer, op. cit., pp 142–3

41 Ibid., p 143

42 British aid to Mihailović was withdrawn at the beginning of 1944 when it was quite clear that he was not aiding his allies, that his men were fighting with the Germans, that he was waiting to come in on the winning side at the end of the war in the hope of re-establishing Serb hegemony

43 See W.S. Churchill, *The Second World War*, vol. v, London, 1952, p 409

44 Sir Winston Churchill gives an account of what he called the 'marvellous resistance' of the Partisans, op. cit., pp 408 et seq.

45 Killed during the German attack on Drvar in 1944. He was the father of a famous young communist killed during the war, Lola Ribar

46 F. Maclean, *Eastern Approaches*, London, 1949, p 313

47 Jovanović, Zujović and Djilas are the three outstanding leaders who turned against Tito after the war

48 Two British officers were with Tito's H.Q. at this time; one of them was killed in the fifth offensive

49 See W.S. Churchill, op. cit., p 412

50 Yugoslav communists' complaints against the Soviet Union were not made public until the Yugoslav-Russian split in 1948. See M. Pijade, *About the Legend that the Yugoslav Uprising owed its Existence to Soviet Assistance*, London, 1950

51 See V. Dedijer, op. cit., pp 215–20, and F. Maclean, op. cit., pp 450–4

4 REVOLUTION AND AFTER

52 *Constitution of the Federative Peoples' Republic of Yugoslavia* (in English translation), Belgrade, 1947

53 *Pregled Istorije SKJ*, op. cit., p 464

54 Full texts of these letters translated into English were published by the Royal Institute for International Affairs in *The Soviet-Yugoslav Dispute*, London, 1948

55 Tito's speech to the Sixth Congress of the Communist Party of Yugoslavia, Zagreb, 3–7 November 1952; in English, Belgrade, 1953, p 11

56 See J.B. Tito, *Report of the Central Committee*, op. cit., pp 128–36

57 *New Fundamental Law of Yugoslavia* (English translation), published by the Union of Jurists of Yugoslavia, Belgrade, 1953

58 A good detailed and objective study of the development of local government in Yugoslavia was undertaken by D.T.B. Scott, and a part of his results has been published in the *Journal of African Administration*, July 1954. I am indebted to Mr Scott for allowing me to see his papers and use his material as one of the bases for the account of local government given in this chapter

59 Official statement of 27 January 1964; figures quoted from report to the National Assembly by Minister of the Interior, V. Lukić

60 All references are to *The Constitution of the Socialist Federal Republic o, Yugoslavia* (English translation), Belgrade, 1963. A new legal code was issued in 1961

61 The right of recall of deputies has existed under other constitutions and

was exercised on occasion notably in the case of Milovan Djilas in 1958
62 In addition to representatives in central and local government, it is claimed that three-quarters of a million men and women are members of some kind of management committee (e.g. school boards: 140,000, co-operative councils: 130,000, tenants' housing committees: 260,000)
63 *Programme of the Yugoslav League of Communists*, 1959, p 157. See also I. Lapenna, *State and Law; Soviet and Yugoslav Theory*, London, 1964

5 ECONOMIC PLANNING AND INDUSTRIAL REVOLUTION

64 *The Law on the Five Year Plan* (English translation), Belgrade, 1947
65 A Yugoslav term meaning value of production and services in industry, forestry, construction, transport, commerce, catering, tourism and crafts, but not including the value of government services, health, insurance, cultural and scientific or professional work
66 Figures from *Economic Survey of Yugoslavia*, May 1962, published by the Organization for Economic Co-operation and Development, Paris, 1962, A. Waterston, *Planning in Yugoslavia*, Baltimore, 1962, and the monthly publications of the Yugoslav Federal Institute for Statistics

6 THE EVOLUTION OF WORKERS' COUNCILS

67 J.B. Tito, *Workers Manage Factories*, Belgrade, 1950, p 34; the text of a speech given to the Federal Assembly, 26 June 1950, on the occasion of the passing of the law establishing Workers' Councils
68 Ibid., p 35
69 The word 'enterprise' is used to cover all businesses (great and small), factories, workshops – any kind of organized work for profit
70 Ibid., pp 47–54. It is now incorporated into the 1963 Constitution
71 Ibid., p 52
72 Ibid., pp 53, 54
73 See F. Singleton and A. Topham, *Workers' Control in Yugoslavia* (Fabian Research Series, No 233), London, 1963, p 15
74 See R. Bićanić, *National Income Distribution in Yugoslavia*, Zagreb, 1955, p 14
75 'Workers' Management in Yugoslavia; a comment', in *Journal of Political Economy*, April 1959, vol LXVII, No 2, pp 197–8
76 V. Dedijer, op. cit., p 18
77 Prior to 1963 there were fourteen different unions; membership figures given are for 1962 – changes in union organization were being made in 1963 and early 1964, so the figures given here are subject to change
78 See F. Singleton and A. Topham, op. cit., p 14

79 V. Dedijer, op. cit., pp 19, 20

80 1 hectare= 2·47 acres

81 See D. Warriner, *Urban Thinkers and Peasant Policy*, op. cit., pp 68 et seq.

82 Ibid., and see J. B. Tito, *Political Report to the Fifth Congress of the Communist Party of Yugoslavia*, 1948, p 122

83 A short study of land utilization in a Slovene village (with an interesting map showing fragmented holdings and widely scattered strips) is to be found in R. F. Cunningham, 'A Land Utilisation Mapping Experiment in Yugoslavia', *Institute of Education Bulletin*, University of Nottingham, October 1963, pp 8–12

84 Peak figures were those for 1957 (6,797 co-operatives with 2 million members) but a number of these co-operatives existed only on paper, and were never effectively organized

85 The remaining hectares (nearly 47,000) were assigned to special purposes such as food production for workers' canteens, etc.

86 Statistics come from the *Statistical Pocket Book of Yugoslavia*, Federal Institute of Statistics, Belgrade, 1963 and 1964

87 Yugoslav sources estimate population losses in the Second World War as 1,700,000, which is 10·7 per cent of an estimated population in March 1941 of 15,970,000

88 *Indeks No 9*, Institute of Statistics, Belgrade, 1963, pp 44, 45

89 *Statistical Pocket Book*, op. cit., pp 90–6

90 1963 Constitution, op. cit., p 3

91 The 1953 census, Institute of Statistics, Belgrade, 1953, listed minorities totalling about 10,000 and including Albanians, Germans, Hungarians, Italians and Turks. The right for cultural use of, and education in their own language, is guaranteed by the constitution and appears to be scrupulously enforced

92 The exchange rate was given as 750 dinars= 1 US dollar

93 He was made a Cardinal in 1953 but never went to Rome to receive his hat. He died of leukaemia in 1960

94 Figures quoted from R. Vidić, *The Position of the Church in Yugoslavia*, Belgrade, 1962, p 63

95 Ibid., pp 48–58

96 Ibid., pp 88–91

97 See M. Djilas, *The New Class; an Analysis of the Communist System*, London, 1957, and *Anatomy of a Moral*, London, 1959

98 Official figures for 1962: see *Statistical Pocket Book*, op. cit., 1963, pp 190, 191

99 These facts about the organization of communists in Yugoslavia are taken from I. Laca and M. Grujić, *The League of Communists in Yugoslavia*, Belgrade, 1960

100 Ibid., p 13

101 Ibid., p 58

102 Ibid., pp 54 et seq.

103 Ibid., p 54

104 Ibid., p 53

105 Tito's own account of his life (especially interesting on its Second World War period) is given in V. Dedijer, op. cit.

List of Abbreviations

AVNOJ	The Anti-Fascist Council of Peoples' Liberation of Yugoslavia
HSS	Hrvatska Seljačka Stranka (formerly the Croat Peasant Party)
IMRO	Internal Macedonian Revolutionary Organization
LYC	League of Communists of Yugoslavia
NRPJ	Nezavisna Radnička Partija Jugoslavije (Independent Workers' Party)
OTKUP	Odelenje Kupiti Ukupno Produkt (Government organization for compulsory purchase of agricultural produce)
UDBa	Uprava Državne Bezbednosti (Secret Police)
UNRRA	United Nations Relief and Rehabilitation Administration
YCP	Yugoslav Communist Party

Select Bibliography

HISTORY BEFORE 1914

Barker, E., *Macedonia: its place in Balkan power politics*, London, 1950

Brailsford, H. N., *Macedonia: its races and their future*, London, 1906

Clissold, S. (ed), *Yugoslav Handbook* (revised edition), Cambridge, 1965

Dvornik, F., *The Slavs: their early history and civilization*, Boston, 1956

Evans, Sir A., *Travels through Bosnia and Hercegovina*, London, 1876

Gardner Wilkinson, Sir J., *Dalmatia and Montenegro*, 2 vols, London, 1848

Heppell, M., and Singleton, F. B., *Yugoslavia*, London, 1961

Jackson, T. G., *Dalmatia, The Quarnero and Istria*, 3 vols, Oxford, 1887

May, A. J., *The Hapsburg Monarchy 1867–1914*, Cambridge, Mass., 1951

Obolensky, D., *The Bogomils*, Cambridge, 1948

Ostrogorsky, G., *History of the Byzantine State* (trans. J. Hussey), Oxford, 1956, Princeton, N.J., 1957

Preveden, F. R., *History of the Croatian People*, Chicago, 1949

Seton Watson, R. W., *The Southern Slav Question and the Hapsburg Monarchy*, London, 1911

Sugar, P., *Industrialization of Bosnia-Hercegovina, 1878–1914*, Washington, 1963

Temperley, Sir H., *History of Serbia*, London, 1919

Vucinich, W. S., *Serbia between East and West: the events of 1903–1908*, Stanford, Cal., 1954

Whelpton, E., *Dalmatia*, London, 1954, London and New York, 1956

Wilkinson, H. R., *Maps and Politics: A Review of the Ethnographic Cartography of Macedonia*, Liverpool, 1951

HISTORY OF THE YUGOSLAV KINGDOM

Baerlein, H., *The Birth of Yugoslavia*, London, 1922

Buchan, J. (ed.), *Yugoslavia*, London, 1923

Kerner, R.J., and Howard, H.N., *The Balkan Conference and the Balkan Entente 1930–1935*, California, 1935

Lederer, I. J., *Yugoslavia at the Paris Peace Conference; a study in frontier-making*, Yale, 1963

Maček, V., *In the Struggle for Freedom*, New York, 1957

Ostovic, P.D., *The Truth about Yugoslavia*, New York, 1952

Pribicevic, S., *Livingspace*, London, 1940

Seton Watson, H., *Eastern Europe between the Wars, 1918–1941*, Cambridge, 1945

Tomasevich, J., *Peasants, Politics and Economic Change in Yugoslavia*, Stanford, 1955

THE SECOND WORLD WAR, 1941–45

Davidson, B., *Partisan Picture*, London, 1946

Dedijer, V., *With Tito through the War, 1941–1944*, London, 1951
Tito Speaks, London, 1953

Maclean, Sir F., *Eastern Approaches*, London, 1950
Disputed Barricade: the Life and Times of Josip Brož-Tito, Marshal of Yugoslavia, London, 1957

Rootham, J., *Miss Fire*, London, 1946

THE YUGOSLAV FEDERAL REPUBLIC 1945 TO 1964

Armstrong, H.F., *Tito and Goliath*, New York, 1951

Betts, R.R. (ed.), *Central and South Eastern Europe 1945–1950*, P. Auty, *Yugoslavia*, London, 1950

Byrnes, R.J., *Yugoslavia*, New York and London, 1949

Degras, J. (ed.), *The Soviet-Yugoslav Dispute*, London, 1948

Kerner, K. (ed.), *Yugoslavia*, California, 1949

Lapenna, I., *State and Law: Soviet and Yugoslav Theory*, London, 1964

Neal, F.W., *Titoism in Action*, California, 1957

Seton Watson, H., *East European Revolution*, London, 1950

Ulam, A.B., *Titoism and the Cominform*, Cambridge, Mass., 1952

MISCELLANEOUS

Ivan Avakumovic, *History of the Communist Party in Yugoslavia*, vol. 1, Univ. of Aberdeen Press, 1964

Djilas, M., *The New Class*, London and New York, 1957
Land Without Justice, London, 1958
Anatomy of a Moral, London and New York, 1959
Conversations with Stalin, London, 1962

227

Durham, E., *Some Tribal Origins, Laws and Customs of the Balkans*, London, 1928

Halpern, J. M., *A Serbian Village*, Oxford and Columbia, New York, 1958

Lodge, O., *Peasant Life in Yugoslavia*, London, 1941

Morrison, W., *Revolt of the Serbs against the Turks* (English translation of heroic poems), Cambridge, 1942

'Organisation for Economic Co-operation and Development', *Yugoslavia*, Paris, 1962 and 1963

Parry, M., and Lord A., *Serbo-Croation Heroic Songs*, 2 vols, Cambridge, Mass., 1954

Trouton, R., *Peasant Renaissance in Yugoslavia, 1900–1950*, London, 1952

Waterston, A., *Planning in Yugoslavia*, Baltimore, 1962

West, R., *Black Lamb and Grey Falcon*, 2 vols, London, 1942

OFFICIAL PUBLICATIONS OF THE YUGOSLAV GOVERN-MENT (IN ENGLISH)

Pamphlets and booklets are available in English on almost every aspect of present-day Yugoslavia. The following is only a small selection from the material available.

The Communist Party of Yugoslavia in the Struggle for New Yugoslavia, for Peoples' Authority, and for Socialism: report delivered by Edward Kardelj at the Vth Congress of the CPY, Belgrade, 1948

Constitution of the Federative Peoples' Republic of Yugoslavia, Belgrade, 1947

The Constitution of the Socialist Federal Republic of Yugoslavia, Belgrade, 1963

Five Year Plan, Belgrade, 1947

The League of Communists of Yugoslavia by Ivan Laca and Momčilo Grujić, Belgrade, 1960

The Liberation Struggle of the Yugoslav Peoples, Belgrade, 1961

New Fundamental Law of Yugoslavia, Belgrade, 1953

Political Report of the Central Committee of the Communist Party of Yugoslavia: report delivered by Josip Brož-Tito at the Vth Congress of the CPY, Belgrade, 1948

Programme of the League of Yugoslav Communists, Belgrade, 1958

Statute of the Socialist Alliance of the Working People of Yugoslavia, Belgrade, 1960

Ten Years of Workers' Management, by S. Vukmanović-Tempo, Belgrade, 1961

Workers Manage Factories in Yugoslavia: speech by Marshal Tito, Belgrade, 1950

Who's Who

ANDRIĆ, Ivo, b. 1892. Historical novelist. Nobel prize for literature 1961. Before Second World War a career diplomat in Yugoslav foreign service. Many of his works are about the past history of his native Bosnia under Turkish occupation.

ANDRASSY, Count Julius (1823–90). Hungarian by birth. Career diplomat in Austria-Hungary. Hungary's first constitutional premier (1867) and Austro-Hungarian Foreign Minister 1871–9. Representative of Austria-Hungary at the Treaty of Berlin 1878 and was responsible for the Austrian occupation of Bosnia-Hercegovina as a result of that treaty.

BULATOVIĆ, Miodrag, b. 1930. Contemporary writer; first novel published in 1956. Best known work in English translation, *The Red Cockerel* (trans. E. D. Goy, 1963).

CINCAR-MARKOVIĆ, Alexander (1889–1948). Career diplomatist in Yugoslavia during period between the two wars. Minister for Foreign Affairs in Cvetković government 1939 and supporter of pro-axis policy.

CVETKOVIĆ, Dragiša, b. 1893. Became Premier of Yugoslavia in 1939 after the fall of Stojadinović and was one of the signatories of the Tripartite Pact with the axis 25 March 1941. Now living in Paris.

CYRIL, Saint (*c.* 826–69). Originally called Constantine, son of a Greek officer in the Byzantine army. Librarian and teacher at the Imperial School at Constantinople. Christian missionary to Slavs who invented written script for slavonic tongue (later to be called glagolitic), into which scriptures and Orthodox liturgy were translated. Missionary work to Khazan and with his brother Methodius in Balkans and Moravia. Assumed name of Cyril on becoming a monk and died in Rome (*see also* Methodius).

DAVIČO, Oskar, b. 1909. Communist writer.

229

DELČEV, Goce (1872–1906). A Macedonian trained as a teacher. Became one of the founders of IMRO and devoted his life to terrorist activities on account of which he himself was killed in 1906.

DJAKOVIĆ, Djuro (1886–1929). A Bosnian metal worker. Engaged in political work in Bosnia; one of the founders of Yugoslav Communist Party 1919 and a communist member of parliament 1920. Became secretary of clandestine YCP 1929 and killed by police whilst under arrest.

DIOCLETIAN (c. 243–316). Born at Dioclea near Salona in Dalmatia; son of Illyrian peasant, rose through ranks of Roman army to high military rank; gained distinction in Persian wars. Chosen by troops to be Emperor 284. Re-organized empire into four divisions to counter barbarian attacks. 305 retired to palace at Split where he died. Last years marked by persecution of Christians which ceased at his death.

DJILAS, Milovan, b. 1911. A Montenegrin. In 1929 became a student at Belgrade University and three years later joined the YCP for which he was sen-tenced to three years imprisonment in 1933. On Tito's reorganization of YCP 1938 became a member of the Central Committee and later of the Politburo and was one of outstanding leaders close to Tito during the Partisan fighting. 1944 Chief of Yugoslav Military Mission to USSR. A member of post-war government being Minister without portfolio, Speaker of the Chamber of Deputies and Vice-President of Yugoslavia. In 1947 took part in foundation of Cominform. Development of his political ideas away from those of Yugoslav communism led to disagreement with YCP leadership in 1953; 1954 expelled from central committee and party and sentenced (1955) to three years imprison-ment; sentence suspended but enforced the following year because he continued to publish anti-communist ideas for which in 1957 he was sentenced to seven years imprisonment. Released conditionally 1961 and rearrested for continuing to publish abroad in 1962.

DRAŠKOVIĆ, Milorad (1873–1921). Minister of the Interior in the provisional government of the Kingdom of Yugoslavia 1920-1. Took harsh measures against all anti-government demonstrations and specially against communists. Retired in 1921 after unsuccessful attempt on his life; assassinated later the same year by a communist said not to have been acting under official party orders.

DUŠAN, Stephen, Emperor of Serbia (1308–55). The last of the Nemanjić family, and the greatest to rule the Serbian kingdom. Extended territory of

Serbia by conquest especially southwards into Macedonia at expense of the Byzantine Empire. Famous for codification of customary law of Serbia known as Code of Stephen Dušan. Became King of Serbia 1331 and caused himself to be crowned Emperor 1346.

FRANZ FERDINAND, Archduke (1863–1914). Member of Habsburg ruling family of Austria-Hungary. Heir to his uncle Franz Josef but more favourable than him to idea of South Slav autonomy within the empire. Murdered whilst on official visit to Sarajevo, capital of Austrian annexed province of Bosnia-Hercegovina in 1914.

GORKIĆ, Milan (alias Josip Čižinski) (c. 1890–c. 1937). His father was a Ukrainian born in Austrian Galicia who became an Austrian civil servant working in Sarajevo (after 1879) where Milan was born. A founding member of the YCP and its representative at the Comintern meetings in the nineteen-twenties. Secretary of clandestine YCP 1932–7 but spent most of his time outside Yugoslavia in Vienna, Moscow, etc. Not trusted by Tito who knew him in these years and fell into disgrace in 1937 and disappeared, presumed dead in the Stalinist purges after 1937.

GROL, Milan (1876–1952). Serbian journalist and politician. One of founders of Serbian Democrat Party in opposition to dictatorship of King Alexander. A member of the *coup d'état* government of General Simović 1941 and in emigra-tion during the war. Co-operated with Tito in provisional government in 1945 becoming one of its Vice-Presidents but resigned before 1945 election and thereafter lived in retirement in Belgrade.

GRUEV, Damian (1871–1906). A Macedonian who worked closely with Goce Delčev and became one of the leaders of IMRO until he was killed in 1906.

HEBRANG, Andrija (c. 1900–1949?). A Croat who joined YCP before the Second World War and later became secretary for its branch in Croatia. After occupation of Croatia and its domination by Pavelić, Hebrang helped to organize Partisan movement; captured and imprisoned by Ustaše. Said to have been tortured and later accused by Tito régime of having agreed to be secret agent for Ustaše. Exchanged by Pavelić régime for Ustaše officers captured by Partisans. After 1945 appointed Minister of Industry and President of Planning Commission but never enjoyed Tito's full confidence. Accused of siding with USSR in the Cominform dispute and arrested 1948. Known to have died shortly after; some reports say by execution, others say by suicide. True facts of his career are difficult to ascertain.

IVANČIĆ, Ljubo, b. 1921. Contemporary Yugoslav painter.

JELLAČIĆ, Josip Count (1801–59). National hero in Croatia of which he was *Ban* (Governor) at the time of the liberation of the serfs in 1848. Helped Austria to suppress Magyar revolt 1848 after Kossuth had refused to promise freedom for Croatia. Stayed on as Ban after 1851 and encouraged Croat separatist movement.

JOVANOVIĆ, Arso (*c*. 1905–48). A Montenegrin. Former Captain (regular) in Royal Yugoslav army. During Second World War joined the Partisans and became Tito's Chief of Staff (to 1946). He took the Soviet line during the Cominform dispute with Yugoslavia and was reputedly shot whilst trying to escape from Yugoslavia to Rumania.

JOVANOVIĆ, Dragoljub, b. 1895. Founded in 1940 the (Serbian) Peoples' Peasant Party of radical but non-communist inspiration, and propagated his ideas in numerous publications. Was a Professor of Belgrade University. Took no part in resistance during the war but afterwards attempted to co-operate with Tito's régime, and was appointed General Secretary of the Narodni Front after 1945. But was critically opposed to communist measures and arrested, tried and imprisoned in 1947. Now living in Belgrade.

KALEB, Vjekoslav, b. 1905. Contemporary writer.

KARADJORDJE (Djordje Petrović) (1752–1817). Leader of the Serbian revolt 1804. Fled to Austria when revolt crushed by Turks 1812. Murdered (with connivance of Miloš Obrenović) on his return to Serbia 1817. Founder of Karadjordjević dynasty.

KARADJORDJEVIĆ, Alexander (1888–1934). Son of Peter I, King of Serbia. Educated officers' school St Petersburg and Serbia. Regent for his father during First World War; succeeded 1921 becoming King of Serbs, Croats and Slovenes later called Yugoslavia. An ardent Serb nationalist who pursued centralist pro-Serbian policy whilst King of Yugoslavia and ruled as dictator without constitution 1928–34. Murdered at Marseilles 1934.

KARADJORDJEVIĆ, King Peter I (1844–1921). Lived in exile in Montenegro, Russia, Switzerland etc., during reigns of Obrenović family. Succeeded as King of Serbia on assassination of Alexander (last of Obrenović family), in 1903. Considered to have had prior knowledge of plot which resulted in assassination. As king dominated by regicides.

KARADJORDJEVIĆ, King Peter II, b. 1923. Became king on his father's assassination in 1934 but rule was by regent Prince Paul. Declared of age to rule by *coup d'état* 27 March 1941. Left Yugoslavia 15 April 1941 after German invasion and never returned. Deposed after election 29 November 1945 when country declared a republic.

KARADJORDJEVIĆ, Prince Paul, b. 1893. Cousin of King Alexander, after whose death in 1934 became regent for King Peter II, a position which he held until the *coup d'état* of 1941 which forced him into exile.

KARADJIĆ, Vuk Stefanović (1787–1864). Father of modern Serbian literature. Took part in 1804 rebellion, tutor to children of Karadjordje. Published many collections of Serbian tales and ballads making written record of oral literature, creating written language of Serbian vernacular, and founding standardized orthography in cyrillic alphabet. Serbo-German dictionary 1818; ethnographic annual Danica 1834. Translated New Testament into reformed Serbian language. His work and reforms are of major and lasting importance though he was much opposed during his lifetime.

KARDELJ, Edward, b. 1910. A Slovene schoolteacher who worked with YCP before Second World War, spent some time in Soviet Union and worked with Tito to reorganize party on eve of war. Always close to Tito and the outstanding theoretician of YCP. With Partisans throughout war; 1942 Vice-President of AVNOJ and continuously Vice-President since Tito's first government although he has also held other positions. Has been closely associated with theory behind all constitutional and party changes and developments. Generally considered a likely successor to Tito.

KRALJEVIĆ, Marko (1335–94). Legendary Serbian hero, son of Vukašin king of West Macedonia of which he became king in succession 1371. Reputed to have fought both with and against Turks, and was Turkish vassal in latter years of reign. His exploits (legendary) celebrated in famous cycle of national Serbian ballads.

KRLJEŽA, Miroslav, b. 1893. Writer, dramatist, critic and left-wing polemicist. A Croat who writes about his native Croatia. Vice-President Yugoslav Academy of Arts and Sciences. Among his best known works *The Return of Philip Latinović* (novel), *Ballad of Petrica Kerempuh and Glembaj* (cycle of plays).

LALIĆ, Mihailo, b. 1914. Communist writer; editor *Borba* 1946–55.

LJOTIĆ, Dimitrije (1891–1945). Lawyer who held office during dictatorship of King Alexander. Head of collaborationist movement which worked with Germans during their occupation of Yugoslavia. Killed in 1945 whilst attempting to escape from Yugoslavia during German retreat.

MAČEK, Vladko (1879–1964). Supporter of Croat Peasant Party of which he became leader after death of Stephen Radić. Doctor of Law; served in Austrian army during First World War. Served several terms of imprisonment for his work in HSS. Signed the agreement (for Croat participation in government) with Prince Paul 26 August 1939 and accepted position of Vice-President. Held this position also in Simović government after *coup d'état* of 27 March 1941. Before invasion had been negotiating with Italians allegedly with a view to getting a separate Croat state. Stayed in Croatia throughout Second World War and went into exile in 1945 first to Paris, later United States.

MACLEAN, Sir Fitzroy Bart., M.P., b. 1911. Sent to Yugoslavia by Sir Winston Churchill during Second World War to be head of British Military Mission with Tito's Partisans. Remained at Tito's HQ until the end of the war. His experiences in Yugoslavia written up in *Eastern Approaches*, London, 1948.

MARKOVIĆ, Sima (1888–1936). A Serb. Professor at Belgrade University. Joined YCP which he helped to found and of which he became joint party secretary 1920–1. Attended Comintern meetings 1918–21. Imprisoned in Yugoslavia for political activities 1922–4. Restored as party secretary on orders of Comintern but fell from favour for right wing deviationism and demoted from office 1928. He was later summoned to Moscow and disappeared during Stalin purges 1936–7.

MARKOVIĆ, Svetozar (1846–75). Political writer and journalist of radical socialist views. Influenced by writing of Marx and his followers and in turn had powerful influence on left wing political thinking in Serbia.

MAŽURANIĆ, Ivan (1814–90). Croat poet associated with national renaissance after 1848.

MEŠTROVIĆ, Ivan (1883–1962). Famous Croat sculptor and nationalist. Associated with struggle for freedom of Croatia before First World War. Died in United States but never severed relations with Tito régime. His works on permanent exhibition in Split, Zagreb and other places in Yugoslavia.

METHODIUS, Saint (825–85). Brother of Saint Cyril (*qv*) son of Byzantine officer lived part of life in Salonica. Accompanied his brother on missionary mission to Slavs. Became Bishop of Syrmia in Pannonia with province in district of valleys Sava, Drava and Raab. His position contested by German Bishops. Visited Rome twice in 868 and in 879 when he was reproved for holding service in Slavonic language but in 880 given permission to do this.

MIHAILOVIĆ, Dragoljub (Draža) (1890–1946). Regular officer in Royal Yugoslav Army. Became leader of resistance movement in Serbia after Yugoslav capitulation in 1941. Strongly pro-Serb and anti-communist; Minister of War in exiled London Government. Collaborated with Germans for which he was tried and executed by Tito's Government 1946.

NEDIĆ, Milan (1887–1946). Chief of Staff and Minister of War in royalist Yugoslav government before Second World War. Collaborated with Germans and appointed by them President of Serbian puppet government after German conquest and occupation of Yugoslavia. Died in prison in Yugoslavia 1946.

NEMANJIĆ family (1168–1371). Rulers of independent medieval Serbian state. First heard of as dukes holding land in fief to Byzantine Empire 1168. Grand Duke Stephen extended territory under family rule and left large patrimony to son Stephen the first crowned king of Serbia 1196–1228. The family continued to rule Serbia until the death of its most famous member Emperor Stephen Dušan. Stephen's son Uroš reigned as Emperor of a disintegrating empire 1355–71.

NJEGOŠ, Danilo Petrović (1670–1725). Elected Orthodox Bishop of Montenegro and began long campaign to free Montenegro from Turkish menace. Virtual ruler of Montenegro and received first emissary from Russia of Peter the Great 1710.

NJEGOŠ, Rade Peter II (1813–51). Became ruler of Montenegro (Vladika) 1830 on death of his uncle Peter I. An enlightened ruler who tried against great difficulties to develop his country. A poet whose most famous poem is *The Mountain Wreath* (1847).

OBRENOVIĆ, Alexander (1876–1903). The last of the Obrenović dynasty in Serbia. Succeeded his father who abdicated 1889. Ruled despotically flouting both constitution and political parties. His marriage to commoner and widow Draga Mašin unpopular especially with army. Murdered together with his wife by military conspirators 1903.

OBRENOVIĆ, Milan (1854–1901). Ruler of Serbia 1868–89 (as prince until 1882 after that as king). A man of dissolute and undisciplined character unwilling to be constitutional ruler but incapable of the sustained effort and hard work to be an efficient dictator. Abdicated 1889 but returned to Serbia to dominate son and organize army 1893–5 and 1897–1900.

OBRENOVIĆ, Miloš (1780–1860). Founder of Obrenović dynasty; one of minor leaders of First Serbian revolt and leader of second revolt 1815. Accepted as ruler of quasi-independent Serbia after this date and became first prince ruler of autonomous Serbia 1830. Deposed for tyranny 1839 but recalled to Serbia to be its Prince again 1858–60.

Pašić, Nikola (1845–1925). Leader of Radical Party in Serbia until First World War. Opponent of dictatorial powers of Obrenović family, gave qualified support to Karadjordjević dynasty. Strong pan-Serb and leader of Serbian politicians during First World War. Helped to give pan-Serb character which caused instability of Yugoslav state after 1918.

Pavelić, Ante (1889–1959). Leader of Ustaše Croat fascist movement which was responsible for murder of King Alexander in 1934. Head (Poglavnik) of independent puppet state of Croatia in collaboration with Germans in Second World War, 1941–5. Responsible for fearful atrocities of Ustaše régime. Fled with retreating German army. Died in South America.

Pijade, Moša (1890–1957). Communist writer, artist, politician and leader. One of founders of YCP 1920 and imprisoned for political activities 1925–39. Whilst in gaol influenced many Communists and met Tito of whom he became lifelong friend. Held many offices in Tito's government including from 1954 President of Chamber of Deputies.

Princip, Gavrilo (1895–1918). Bosnian student member of patriotic organization which aimed to free Bosnia-Hercegovina from alien Austrian rule. As a member of conspiracy group shot Archduke Franz Ferdinand of Austria 28 June 1914 during archduke's official visit at Sarajevo. Condemned to rigorous life imprisonment of which he died at the end of the First World War.

Radić, Stephen (1871–1928). With his brother Antun founded Croat Peasant Party (Hrvatska Seljačka Stranka known as HSS) in 1905. Educated in Vienna and Prague; influenced by T. G. Masaryk. In state of Yugoslavia after 1918 stood out for Croat autonomy and against Serbian centralism. Collaborated briefly with Pašić (1925) and also briefly with Communist Peasant International. Shot during session of Serbian parliament in 1928 and died shortly afterwards. Much revered by Croat peasants amongst whom he had worked for so long.

Ranković, Alexander, b. 1903. A member of YCP since 1928. Imprisoned before Second World War for political activities but released and associated with Tito in reorganization of party on eve of war. One of Tito's closest associates during and since war. Minister of Interior in Tito's government

1946–53. Became Vice-President 1953 and has remained one of most important leaders of present-day Yugoslavia whose name is considered with that of Kardelj as possible successor to Tito.

RIBAR, Ivan, b. 1881. A Serbian lawyer, President of Yugoslavia Constituent Assembly 1921 and Vice-President of Serbian Democrat Party. Joined the Partisans during the war. His two sons were prominent communists in Partisan movement and both lost their lives. President of A V N O J and of provisional parliament 1945. President of Yugoslavia 1945–53.

RISTIĆ, Marko, b. 1902. Contemporary communist writer; 1945–51 ambassador in Paris for Yugoslav government.

SAVA, Saint (c. 1174–1235). The youngest son of Grand Duke Stephen Nemanjić. Called Rastko until he became a monk at Athos where he founded Serbian monastery of Hilandar. Founder and first Archbishop of the independent Serbian Orthodox Church. Did much to help the establishment of early kingdom of Serbia.

SIMOVIĆ, Dušan (1882–1962). General Commander of Yugoslav Air Force before 27 March 1941 *coup d'état* which deposed Regent Prince Paul and declared King Peter II of age naming General Simović as Premier. Held this position until defeat of Royal Yugoslav army by the Germans. Went into exile with King and other members of government. Held positions in *émigré* government (though superseded as premier) but returned to Yugoslavia after the end of the war living in Belgrade in pensioned retirement until his death.

STAMBULIĆ, Peter, b. 1912. Leading Yugoslav communist member of Central Committee of L Y C. President of Parliament 1957 and of Serbian Republican Parliament 1963. A Serb considered to be one of most important personalities in present communist leadership.

STARČEVIĆ, Ante (1823–96). Son of Orthodox father and Catholic mother, born in Croatia. At first a supporter of the Illyrian movement but later developed strong feelings of Croatian nationalism and came to make exaggerated claims for a greater Croatia.

STEPINAC, Aloysius, Archbishop (1890–1960). A Croat. Mobilized into Austrian army in First World War; supported formation of Yugoslav state. Appointed Archbishop of Zagreb 1937 and Cardinal 1953 but did not go to Rome to receive his Cardinal's hat. Remained in Zagreb during Second World War. Outspoken critic of the communist nature of Tito's régime. 1946 charged with wartime collaboration and sentenced to sixteen years imprisonment but conditional release in 1951. Died of leukaemia 1960.

STOJADINOVIĆ, Milan (1888–1961). Serbian politician of inter-war years. Collaborated with Prince Paul during regency and became Premier 1935 to 1938. Used his position to amass great wealth and large estates. Friend of Nazis and Fascists and fell from power on suspicion of aiming to become Yugoslav Führer; imprisoned 1940 and handed over to British Authorities by Simović government after 27 March 1941. Imprisoned by allies in Mauritius during Second World War after which, on regaining his freedom, settled in Argentina.

STROSSMEYER, Josip Juraj, Bishop (1815–1905). Liberal Catholic Bishop of Djakovo. A believer in union between Catholic and Orthodox Churches, supporter of South Slav union and of the idea of autonomy for South Slavs within the Austro-Hungarian Empire. Patron of liberal culture especially in Croatia. 1867 founding member of Academy of Arts and Science in Zagreb and 1874 of University of Zagreb. Encountered much hostility from Catholics and Orthodox, from Croats, Serb, Austrians and many others on account of his liberal views. A friend of Croat historian Rački and correspondent of British statesman, Gladstone.

ŠUBAŠIĆ, Ivan (1892–1955). Leading member of Croat Peasant Party between the two wars. Became Ban of Croatia after the Cvetković-Maček agreement about Croatian autonomy 1941. As Premier of Yugoslav Royalist government in exile negotiated Tito-Šubašić agreement and became Foreign Minister in Tito's provisional government but resigned before the 1945 election in Yugoslavia and thence forward lived in retirement in Croatia.

SUPILO, Frano (1870–1917). A disciple and supporter of ideas of Trumbić with whom he was associated in founding the Yugoslav Committee during First World War and organizing support for Yugoslav idea.

ŠUTEJ, Juraj, b. 1889. Jurist and politician. Leading member of Croat Peasant Party. Minister of Finance in Cvetković cabinet 1939 to 1941 and held office in all *émigré* Royalist governments during the war. With Subašić attempted to work with Tito and was Minister of Trade and Industry in his provisional government 1944–5. Resigned before 1945 election. Living in retirement in Zagreb.

TITO, Josip Brož, b. 1892. Inspiration and creator of communist republic of Yugoslavia. Marshal, President, Supreme Commander of armed forces, member of parliament (for Belgrade), General Secretary of Y C P. Member of Academies of Yugoslavia in Belgrade, Zagreb and Ljubljana; Hon. Doctor of Rangoon University.

Brought up in Catholic family (Slovene mother, Croat father) in Kumrovec, Croatian Zagorje in conditions of poverty. Educated at village school. Became apprentice and later qualified metal worker and joined trade union of his craft which he practised in Austria and Germany. Conscripted to Austrian army in First World War and became N C O. Taken prisoner by Russians on eastern front 1915, wounded and hospitalized and imprisoned in Russia where he remained until 1920 seeing something of (but not actively participating in) Russian revolution. Returned to Croatia 1920 and joined Y C P. Imprisoned for political activities. After release became member of Politburo 1934. 1934–7 working for Comintern in Moscow and various countries of Europe after which appointed to reorganize and clean up disintegrated Y C P on which he was engaged (after various activities connected with sending volunteers to Spain during Spanish Civil War) until outbreak of Second World War. After 1941 prepared Y C P to organize fighting when time considered ripe; signal for uprising given by Tito to Y C P as soon as U S S R was attacked by Germany. Leader of Resistance Movement (Partisans) from July 1941 to end of war. Received help from allies because he organized active resistance to Germans and their assistants and continued to collaborate with Russians from whom he received advice but little help. Organized Communist republican government of Yugoslavia after war. 1945–53 Premier and Minister of National Defence. 1953 President of Yugoslavia. 1963 appointed President for life. Three times married, present wife Jovanka Brož-Tito. Two children. Many speeches, articles and political statements have been published.

TKALAC, Imbro Ignatijević (1824–1912). Writer of strong liberal principles who edited periodicals in Zagreb and Vienna, and finally lived in exile (Official of Italian Ministry of Foreign Affairs) because of his political principles and strong Croatian views made him suspect to AustroHungarian Government in Croatia. His autobiography *Jugenderrinerungen aus Kroatien* (*Memories of youth in Croatia*) published in Leipzig 1891 (and not in Croatia till 1924) a powerful and evocative description of feudal life in Croatia before peasants gained some freedom in 1848.

TRUBAR, Primož (1508–86). A Slovene Church reformer and writer during Reformation period.

TRUMBIĆ, Ante (1864–1938). A Croat from Dalmatia founder of Croatian Social Democrat Party 1895. Drew up Fiume resolution 1905 which pledged

Croats to fight together for freedom. Worked for union of Dalmatia with Croatia and creation of South Slav bloc within Austro-Hungarian Empire. Hoped for trialist autonomy for Croatia, Slavonia, Dalmatia. Helped to organize Yugoslav committee in First World War and for equal rights for Serbs, Croats and Slovenes in a Yugoslav kingdom. Opposed to pan-Serb policy of King Alexander which triumphed after 1918; Foreign Minister in Provisional Yugoslav Government 1918, tireless worker on peace negotiations; retired disappointed with development of new state to private life 1921. One of founders of the Yugoslav state.

ŽUJOVIĆ, Sreten, b. c. 1910. A Serb. Joined YCP and one of chief organizers of uprising in Serbia in summer of 1941. Appointed deputy to Tito as Commander-in-Chief. After war held various important cabinet posts but was disgraced and imprisoned after siding with USSR in Cominform quarrel 1948. Released from prison 1950–1 after recantation and thought to have been reinstated as party member. Working in Belgrade.

Acknowledgements

Agencija za Fotodokumentaciju, Zagreb, 28, 62; Paul Almasy (Camera Press), 81 Arts Council of Great Britain, 11; Associated Press, 24, 34, 35, 40, 43, 44, 55, 56, 57, 73, 89, 90, 91; National Museum, Belgrade, 17; Yugoslav Army Museum, Belgrade, 37, 42, 45, 46, 47, 51; Bosnian Information Service, 66; Camera Press, 48, 50, 59, 67, 70, 75, 80, 81, 92; Centroturist, Zagreb, 2; Njegoš Museum, Cetinje, and Tošo Dabac, 25; Croatian Information Service, 26, 27, 63, 64, 83; Tošo Dabac, 1a, 10, 25; Exportprojekt, Ljubljana, 71; Mladen Grčević, 3, 20, 78; Hirmer Fotoarchiv, Munich, 6; Blasko Jonanović, 65; Ethnographic Museum, Ljubljana, 15; Imperial War Museum, London, 52; Miša Pavlović, 5, 7; Radio Times Hulton Picture Library, 72; Service d'informations Yougoslavie, 60, 61, 85, 86, 88; Archaeological Museum, Skopje, 1b; Dušan Stanimirović, 19; By courtesy of Stvarnost, Zagreb, 33, 38, 39, 49, 53, 54, 76, 93, 94; Tanjug, 4, 9, 30, 36, 41, 77; By courtesy of the Yugoslav Embassy, London, 74, 79, 84, 87; Yugoslav National Tourist Office, London, 8, 12, 16, 22, 68, 69, 82; Vilko Zuber, 14.

Index

Black Hand (Serbian nationalist society), 37
Black market, 136, 174, 175
Black Sea, 58
Bled, castle of, 48
Blood feud, 55
Bogomils (Patarines), 14, 49, *12*
Boka Kotorska, 55
Bor copper mines, 78
Borba (Communist newspaper), 82
Bosnia, 14, 28, 38, 44, 45, 49–53, 89, 91, 92, 169
Bosnia-Hercegovina, 7, 11, 81, 195, *22, 23*; autonomous republic of, 25, 107; ceded to Austria-Hungary, 35–7; history up to 1914, 49–53; population in 1918, 72; need for land reform, 77; agriculture in, 173, 175, 177, 188; General Co-operatives in, 175, 182; population structure, 185, 186; illiteracy rate, 186; position of women, 191; Orthodox Church in, 199
Bosnian Moslems, 76
Bosnians, census of, 194
Božić, Mirko, 192
Bratsvo (family ties), 55
Broadcasting stations, 189
Brož, Josip, 83, 91 (*see* Tito)
Budva, 55
Bulatović, Miodrag, 192
Bulganin, Marshal, 121
Bulgaria, 25, 36, 37, 71, 76, 79, 112; and Macedonia, 56–9; receives part of Macedonia, 87
Bulgarian communists, 88
Bulgarian Empire, 57
Bulgars, 12, 60
Byzantine Empire, 10, 11, 25–6, 38, 44, 57

CARINTHIA, 47, 71
Carniola, 40, 47
Catherine the Great, 32
Catholic Church/Catholics, 7, 11, 14, 15, 26, 38, 43, 44, 47, 49, 50, 53, 73, 87, 106; in Croatia; former richness, privilege and influence, 196; census

figures for, 196; and the Communist Party, 197–9
Catholic Slovene People's Party, 48
Cavtat, 10
Celovec, 175
Celts, 10, 13
Četniks, 88–9, 93
Chamber of Producers (second chamber of Yugoslav parliament), 116–17
Chambers of Producers (in local government), 117, 119, 122, 123, 137
China, 121
Church property, 197
Churchill, Winston, 80, 93, *50*
Čiftliks (tenancies), 59
Cincar-Marković (*see* Who's Who: *p.* 229), 80
Claudius, Emperor, *12*
Collectivization, 112, 137, 173
Cominform, 112–14, 116, 195
Comintern, 82–5
Communes, 118, 122, 124
Communist International (*see* Comintern)
Communist Manifesto (Marx), 171
Communist Party of Yugoslavia (later League of Communists), 105, 144, *49*; outlawed in 1920, 74, 81–2; origins, 81; split into warring factions, 82–5; effect of Stalin's purge on, 85; Tito becomes General Secretary, 85–6; growth of, and support from Russia, 86; resistance activities during Second World War, 88; importance of its role in the War, 104; and the immediate post-war period, 105–6; adapts Russian institutions, 109, 111; maintains secrecy, 111; conflict with USSR, 113–16; under the 1952 constitution, 119–20; and the trade unions, 155, 157; and national unity, 195; and the churches, 196–200; and political power, 209; membership and organization, 212–15
Communists, in Yugoslav parliament of 1920, 73
Constantine the Great, *12*

Murad, Sultan, 28
Mussolini, Benito, 79

NAISSIUS, 12
Naisus (Niš), 12
Naples, 93
Napoleon I, 32, 33, 42, 45
National (later Communal) Bank, 148, 179
National income, 136, 141
National Liberation Movement, 105
Nationalities: Serbo-Croat feuds, 76, 79–80, 106; question of rivalries and national unity, 193–6; Council of, 106, 116
Nationalization, 107, 108, 112
Nazi-Soviet pact, 86
Nazor, Vladimir, 192
Nedić, General Milan (see Who's Who: p. 235), 88, 93
Nemanjić family, of Serbia, 26
Nemanjić kings, 53
Neretva, river, 91
New Fundamental Law, 108, 116
New Zealand Division, in Trieste, 93
Nicholas, Prince (later King) of Montenegro, 54, 69
Niš, 12
Njegoš II, Peter (see Peter)
Normans of Sicily, 38
Novi Pazar, Sanjak of, 28, 54

Oblast (region), 109
Obrenović, Michael, 34
Obrenović, Miloš (see Milos)
Obzana, the, 81
Ohrid, 60; Bishop of, 26
Ohrid, lake, 56, 58
Okrug (circuit), 109
Opština (village government), 109
Orthodox Church/Orthodox Christians, 7, 10, 11, 14, 15, 38, 39, 43, 49, 50, 53, 57, 106; official religion of Serbia, 26; and Serb nationalism, 30–1; the Exarchate, 57; slaughter of, in Croatia, 87, 196; former richness, privilege and

influence, 196; census figures of, 196; and the Communist Party, 197, 199, 90
Ostrogoths, 12
OTKUP (system of obligatory sale), 174–5, 179, 183
Ottoman Empire (see Turkey)

PACTA CONVENTA (1102), 39
Pannonia, 11, 12
Pannonian Croatia, 38
Paris, 85
Parliament of Yugoslavia (see Federal Peoples' Assembly)
Partisans, 78, 104, 105, 192, 193, 43–45; Tito's organization of, 88; differences with Četniks, 89; set up central government, 89–90; British Military mission to, 91; resolutions of their Executive Council, 91–2; their success, 93
Party of Rights (Croatia), 43
Pašić, Nikola (see Who's Who: p. 236), 73
Passarowitz (Požarevac), Treaty of (1718), 32
Paton, A. A., quoted 54
Paul, St, 14
Paul Karadjordjević, Prince of Yugoslavia (see Who's Who: p. 233), 75, 76, 79, 86, 40
Pavelić, Ante (see Who's Who: p. 236), 87, 197–8, 48
Peace Conference (1919), 71
Peasants, 119; census figure of, 169; the old and the new peasantry, 169–70; their food, 170; and private property, 170–2; resettlement of, 173–4; and obligatory sale to the government, 174–5; and co-operative farms, 175–80; new deal for, 180–5; income of self-employed, 188; housing for, 189
Peć, 27, 60
Pečalbari (temporary emigrants), 59
Peoples' Army of Liberation (Partisans, q.v.), 89, 44
Peoples' Committees (savet), 109–10, 118, 119–20, 140, 146, 150, 153, 154
Peoples' Courts, 111

249